W9-BBX-089

# THE Family OF GOD

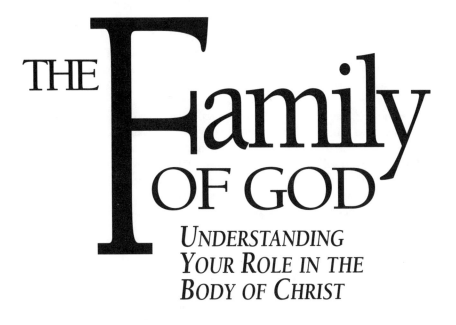

# THE Family OF GOD

### UNDERSTANDING YOUR ROLE IN THE BODY OF CHRIST

## CHARLES R. SWINDOLL

*with study helps by Val Harvey*

**BROADMAN PRESS**
NASHVILLE, TENNESSEE

© 1986 by Charles R. Swindoll, Inc.
Originally published by Multnomah Press
Portland, Oregon 97266
Study questions © 1993 by Broadman Press
**4261-37**
**ISBN: 0-8054-6137-X**
Dewey Decimal Classification: 248.4
Subject Heading: CHRISTIAN LIFE
Printed in the United States of America

Scripture quotations, unless otherwise marked, are from the *New American Standard Bible.* © The Lockman Foundation 1960, 1962, 1963, 1971, 1972, 1973, 1975, 1977. Used by permission.

Scripture references marked NIV are from the Holy Bible, *New International Version,* copyright © 1973, 1978, 1984 by International Bible Society.

Scripture verses marked TLB are taken from *The Living Bible.* Copyright © Tyndale House Publishers, Wheaton, Illinois, 1971. Used by permission.

Scripture references marked AMP are from *The Amplified Bible,* Old Testament. Copyright ©1962, 1964 by Zondervan Publishing House. Used by Permission. *The Amplified New Testament* ©The Lockman Foundation 1954, 1958, 1987. Used by permission.

Scripture references marked GNB are from the *Good News Bible*, the Bible in Today's English Version. Old Testament: Copyright © American Bible Society 1976; New Testament; Copyright © American Bible Society 1966, 1971, 1976. Used by permission.

Scripture references marked Phillips are reprinted with permission of Macmillan Publishing Co., Inc. from J. B. Phillips: *The New Testament in Modern English,* Revised Edition. © J. B. Phillips 1958, 1960, 1972.

Scripture references marked KJV are from the *King James Version* of the Bible.

Scripture references marked MLB are from *The Modern Language Bible, The New Berkeley Version.* Copyright 1945, 1959 © 1969 by Zondervan Publishing House. Used by permission.

This volume is affectionately
dedicated to four faithful men:

---

## Cyril Barber

## Bill Butterworth

## David Lien

## Bill Watkins

---

who serve behind the scenes at Insight
for Living, giving counsel and
encouragement to those who hurt,
finding in Scripture the foundation of
their faith. I am indebted to each man
for his unswerving commitment to
God's truth, his unselfish ministry to
people in need, his unceasing
discipline to stay at an endless task,
and his unsurpassed loyalty to my wife
and me as friends.

# Contents

# Introduction

For years I have wanted to write on doctrine . . . Bible doctrine. My flesh has been willing, but my spirit has been weak. That calls for an explanation.

The need for knowledge of the Scripture is obvious. Everywhere I turn I meet or hear about well-meaning Christians who are long on zeal but short on facts . . . lots of enthusiasm and motivation but foggy when it comes to scriptural truth.

They have a deep and genuine desire to be used by God, to reach the lost, to serve in the church, to invest their energies in "the kingdom of God and His righteousness," but their doctrinal foundation is shifting sand rather than solid rock. The result is predictable: They are at the mercy of their emotions, flying high one day and scraping the bottom the next. A frustrating yo-yo syndrome.

I know. For more years than I care to remember, I, too, climbed and tumbled, soared, and submerged, thought I knew the scoop, then later discovered how off-target I really was. The whole miserable mess leaves a person filled with doubt and disillusionment, grossly lacking in confidence, not to mention having that awful feeling of being exposed. At that point, most Christians decide to pack it in lest they get caught again in a similar position of vulnerability. You and I may be amazed to know how many have retreated into the background scenery of passivity simply because their ignorance of the basic building blocks caused them embarrassment.

Like I said, the need is obvious. Being a fixer-upper type, I am prompted to jump in with both feet and crank out a pile of pages that will provide the doctrinal ammunition so

9

many Christians need. That's why I said my flesh is willing. But since I am also a let's-be-realistic type, I am reluctant.

Among the last things believers need is another dull volume on doctrine. Sterile and unapplied theology interests no one living in the real world. Most of those books wind up as great (and expensive!) doorstops. They also make a good impression when the pastor drops by for a visit and sees them lying there, freshly dusted, on the coffee table. And there is nothing like wading through thick theological works late at night to cure your battle with insomnia. Who hasn't come close to fracturing his nose on an eight-pound volume while trying to make it past page 3 in the prone position?

That's why my spirit is weak. Deep within me has been this growing fear of just pumping out another thick, boring book on doctrine that looks good but reads bad.

### Theology Needs to Be Interesting

Since I am committed to accuracy, clarity, and practicality, I loathe the thought of publishing something that is anything but interesting, easily understood, creative—and yes, even captivating. See why my desire to write a book on doctrine has been on the back burner so long? It isn't easy to communicate the deepest truths of the Bible in an interesting manner. It has taken years for me to be convinced that it can be done . . . and even more years to be convinced that I may be able to do it. The chapters that follow are my best effort at accomplishing this objective. Only time will tell whether I have achieved my desire.

If my stuff makes sense, if the average individual is able to follow my thinking, picture the scenes, grasp my logic, come to similar conclusions, and later pass on a few of those thoughts to someone else, then the book will have made the impact I desired. But if it lacks real substance, or if the reader discovers it requires a graduate degree to track my thoughts, or even if it proves to be true to the biblical text yet comes across as tedious and pedantic, then my face, I can assure you, will be as red as your nose.

*Introduction*

## The Need to Improve Theology's Reputation

Frankly, theology has gotten a bum rap. Just ask around. Make up a few questions and try them on for size in your church. You'll see. Many folks, if they are candid with you, will confess a distaste for sound biblical doctrines. Sound theology, like Rodney Dangerfield, "don't get no respect." You question that? Then let me suggest you do your own personal survey among some Christians. Ask things like:

- Ever made a study of the doctrines in the Bible?
- How would you respond if your pastor announced plans to bring a series of pulpit messages on several "important theological subjects"?
- Do you believe that all Christians ought to know where they stand doctrinally, or is that more the business of the clergy?
- When you hear the word *theology*, do you have a mental image of something interesting and stimulating? Or do you honestly think, *Dull stuff . . . please don't bore me?*
- On a scale of one to ten (ten being most important), how high would you rate a knowledge of theology?
- Can you remember a doctrinal sermon—or one lesson on theology you were involved in—that you actually *enjoyed*?
- Choosing your preference, rearrange these topics in the order you consider most interesting and timely. Which interests you the most? The least? Give each a number from one to seven.
  - _____ a biographical look at a biblical character
  - _____ a verse-by-verse analysis of a book in the New Testament
  - _____ a serious study of biblical doctrines
  - _____ what God's Word teaches about the home and family
  - _____ moral, social, and ethical issues according to Scripture
  - _____ biblical principles for success and personal motivation

_____ Proverbs made practical for today

Unless you are most unusual, the study of doctrine would be ranked toward the bottom, if not altogether in last place. Compared to success principles on the home and family, "a serious study of biblical doctrines" does not seem nearly as important or relevant to most evangelical congregations. Yet, believe it or not, at the very heart of all those other topics is a great deal of theology.

It is surprising for most Christians to hear that their doctrinal position determines their interpretation and application of Scripture—whether or not they have ever declared themselves doctrinally. What roots are to a tree, the doctrines are to the Christian. From them we draw our emotional stability, our mental food for growth, as well as our spiritual energy and perspective on life itself. By returning to our roots, we determine precisely where we stand. We equip ourselves for living the life God designed for us to live.

## Why Is Doctrine Often So Dull?

If all this is true, then why does the mere mention of theology turn off so many people? Why are most churches full of people programmed to think that doctrine is a synonym for dullness and boredom?

At the risk of appearing ultracritical, I'll be frank with you. Much of the problem lies with theologians who have done a poor job of communicating their subject. No offense, theological scholars, but you are notorious for talking only to yourselves. The language you employ is clergy code-talk, woefully lacking in relevance and reality. The terms you use are in-house jargon, seldom broken down into manageable units for people who aren't clued in. You may be accurate and certainly sincere, but your world is like the television series of yesteryear, "One Step Beyond." Please understand that we love you and respect you. No one would dare to question your brilliance. We need your gifts in the body and we admire your ability to stay at the disciplines of your studies. We just don't understand you.

As a result, much of what you write is kept within those

cloistered chambers that intimidate people who haven't had the privilege of probing the heavenlies as you have. The majority feel a distance from you when you share your secrets. I realize that many of you wish this weren't so, but I suppose it comes with the territory.

In this book and the others in this study series, my hope is to build a bridge of theological understanding with the common man, the uninitiated individual, the person who has never been to seminary—and doesn't care to to go—but really does want to develop a solid network of doctrinal roots.

I'm interested in reaching the truck driver, the athlete, the waitress, the high school student, the person in the military service, the homemaker who has a houseful of kids at her feet, the business person whose world is practical, earthy, tough, and relentless . . . and a hundred other "types" who have the brains to absorb biblical truth but lack the time and patience to look up every sixth or seventh word in a dictionary.

I therefore make no apology for approaching various subjects in a different way than standard theologians. I want everyone who picks up this book to understand every word and grasp every principle, even if you don't agree with them. (To disagree with me is your privilege—I expect it. In fact, I invite it. But to misunderstand or to *fail* to understand what I'm getting at would be tragic.)

I freely confess that I want you to enjoy this journey . . . to find out that discovering doctrine and seeing its importance can encourage you like nothing else. I want us to laugh together, as well as think together, as we dig into *the Book*. It's been my observation for the past twenty-five years of ministry that there is no subject too deep for anyone to understand if the material is presented creatively and clearly, sparked periodically by humor, and accompanied by illustrations that let plenty of life in. All this is true of folks who really want to learn.

By the way, that brings up another reason doctrine is dull to some people. As I implied earlier, they have a built-in, long-standing *prejudice* against it. Somehow, they have convinced themselves that (a) they don't need to fuss around with heady stuff like that since they aren't doing "full-time ministry," or (b) even if they made a study of the doctrines, all that knowledge would be of little practical value. In subtle ways these two excuses tend to plug their ears and clog the learning process.

Without trying to perform an overkill, both of those excuses are totally erroneous. Because every Christian is "doing full-time ministry," being theologically informed and equipped could not be more important. And since when does a knowledge of important facts lack practical value? If I recall Jesus' words correctly, that which makes us free is knowing the truth. It's ignorance that binds us, not knowledge. Furthermore, we are left defenseless before the cults and other persuasive false teachers if we lack this solid network of doctrinal roots. As I stated earlier, it stabilizes us.

## An Approach that Will Keep Things Interesting

Before we get underway, let me explain my plan of approach.

I have no intention of writing an exhaustive theological treatment on all the biblical doctrines. (If you happen to be a perfectionist, expecting every jot and tittle to be addressed in this volume or the others in this series, please read that sentence again.) My plan is to offer a broad-brush approach to most of the essential points of evangelical truth. If you find certain details are not covered to your satisfaction or if you observe that some subjects of interest to you are not even mentioned, just remember that is on purpose. I'm hoping to whet your appetite for a much more intense and thorough study *on your own* once you've begun to get excited about these essential areas. Who knows? Maybe one day *you'll* be the one who will write a more thorough and analytical work. Be my guest.

You'll also want to keep a Bible handy. I'll try to quote as many of the main verses and passages as possible. But there will be times that I will give an additional reference or two which you might want to look up right then. If you have the time, please do that. Before too long you will begin to feel much more at home in the Scriptures. And use a good study Bible rather than a loose paraphrase or a copy of just the New Testament.

There are a number of study tools that make the Bible and its people come to life for you. *Commentaries* explore books of the Bible and tell you what scholars have discovered about the writers of the books, the times in which they lived, and what the Scriptures mean. *Bible encyclopedias, dictionaries,* and *handbooks* contain information about the people, places, and events in the Bible. They often include drawings and pictures to help you put yourself in the first-century world. *Bible atlases* have maps that show how the Holy Land looked at various times throughout history. Atlases usually give background information about governments and geography. *Concordances* tell you where words appear in the Bible. Pick a word like *love*; look it up just like you would in a dictionary; and you'll find a list of verses in which *love* is used. If you're serious about Bible study, you'll want to stop by a bookstore and invest in a good Bible handbook, atlas, and concordance. You'll be surprised how much those resources will add to your study.

At the end of the first chapter of each part of this book you will note several thoughts I call "Root Issues." These are simply practical suggestions designed to help you keep the doctrines out of the realm of sterile theory and in touch with the real world. To get the most out of these, I'd recommend that you purchase a handy-sized spiral notebook—your personal "Root Issues Notebook"—to record your thoughts, observations, and responses. Each chapter concludes with study questions. "Extending Your Roots" helps you explore what we've been talking about. "Taproot" takes you even further in your study of each doctrine. Don't be afraid to write your answers in this book. It's yours—make it personal.

## Ten Major Areas of Doctrine

Finally, the outline I want to follow will be interwoven in this series of five study guides. All the doctrines I want to cover will fall within these ten major categories:

- The Bible
- God the Father
- The Lord Jesus Christ
- The Holy Spirit
- The Depravity of Humanity
- Salvation
- The Return of Christ
- Resurrection
- The Body of Christ
- The Family of God

As I mentioned earlier, the list is purposely not exhaustive, but there is plenty here to get our roots firmly in place. In fact, the better-known historic creeds down through the ages have included these ten areas. While considering this recently, I decided to write my own doctrinal credo, a statement of my personal faith. What it may lack in theological sophistication I have tried to make up for in practical terminology.

As I return to the roots of my faith, I am encouraged to find the time-honored foundations firmly intact:

- I affirm my confidence in God's inerrant Word. I treasure its truths and I respect its reproofs.
- I acknowledge the Creator-God as my Heavenly Father, infinitely perfect, and intimately acquainted with all my ways.
- I claim Jesus Christ as my Lord—very God who came in human flesh—the object of my worship and the subject of my praise.
- I recognize the Holy Spirit as the third member of the Godhead, incessantly at work convicting, convincing, and comforting.
- I confess that Adam's fall into sin left humanity without the hope of heaven apart from a new birth, made possible by the Savior's death and bodily resurrection.
- I believe the offer of salvation is God's love-gift to all. Those who accept it by faith, apart from works, become new creatures in Christ.

*Introduction*

- I anticipate my Lord's promised return, which could occur at any moment.
- I am convinced that all who have died will be brought back from beyond—believers to everlasting communion with God and unbelievers to everlasting separation from God.
- I know the Lord is continuing to enlarge His family, the universal body of Christ, over which He rules as Head.
- I am grateful to be a part of a local church which exists to proclaim God's truth, to administer the ordinances, to stimulate growth toward maturity, and to bring glory to God.

With confidence and joy, I declare this to be a statement of the essentials of my faith.

That's where I stand . . . sort of a preview of coming attractions. Now it's time for you to dig in and discover where you stand. With God's help I think you will find this study one of the most important and interesting projects you have ever undertaken. You may even get so "fanatical" about your faith that your whole perspective on life changes.

Come to think of it, that's exactly what Christianity is supposed to do . . . change our lives.

I wish to thank my long-term, splendid secretary as I have so many times before. Helen Peters has done it again. Without regard for her own needs and preferences, she has deciphered my hand scratching, typed and retyped my manuscript, verified my footnotes, corrected my spelling, and helped me meet my deadlines. "Thank you" seems hardly sufficient to declare the depth of my gratitude. I also want to thank Val Harvey for her excellent work in writing the study questions for each of the volumes in this series.

And now let's dig in. You have stumbled your way through shifting sand long enough. May these books on Bible doctrine give you just the help you need so that you can stand firmly and finally on a foundation that is solid as rock.

Charles R. Swindoll
Fullerton, California

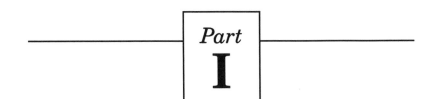

# The Body
# of Christ

# 1 God's Body-Building Program

A typical American family was driving home from church one Sunday. Dad was fussing about the sermon being too long and sort of boring. Mom said she thought the organist played too loudly during the second hymn they sang. Sis, who was a music major in college, said she thought the soloist sang about a half note off-key during most of her song. Grandma said she couldn't hear very well—since they were sitting toward the back. As they pulled in the driveway, little Willie, who had listened to all of this, started to fuss about the woman who sat in front of him with that big hat. Then he paused, nudged his dad, and said, "But, Dad, you gotta admit, it was a pretty good show for a nickel."

Ouch!

To more people than we would dare admit, attending church is a lot like watching a show. The better the entertainment, the more they enjoy coming. But the less they like what they see and hear, the more they grumble and complain. Let the "show" get really bad, and there's no way most people are going to see it through. Yet, we've got to admit that the "price of admission" is still pretty hard to beat. Compared to what the public is willing to pay for live theater or a professional ball game, it's still "a pretty good show for a nickel."

All of this is true, of course, until you get serious about this business of "the church." Things change when you do. You feel less like seeking entertainment. You feel less freedom to fuss and complain. You feel more like investing your time, your treasure—your very life.

As a matter of fact, it isn't long before you realize that this is one of the few involvements you mess around with that has eternal dimensions on earth. And when you *really* get hooked, you discover there is not one other single involvement more important than the Lord's whole-world outreach.

When you stop and think about it, God is involved in only two worldwide construction projects. The first is called *evangelism,* where He stretches His big arms around the world to reach and to win the lost to Himself. He uses all different kinds of people and many different methods, but in every case His objective is to offer the good news of His Son, Jesus Christ, to those who have yet to respond. The scope of God's world program is limitless; it reaches across the street, across the States, and across the seas.

The second worldwide program God is involved in is *the church.* I think of the church as God's body-building program. Do you know the materials He uses for building the church? That's easy to figure out, isn't it? He uses those He recruits in evangelism. So these two programs work in sync with each other. The lost are found as they respond positively to the good news of Christ. Then they begin to be built up in Christ and become personally involved in God's world program. The church's mission is a never-ending project, drawing its manpower (should I say person power?) and its funding from those who have caught the vision.

You need to understand that I am not writing about some local church *per se* or some denomination. I don't have any geographical location in mind either. Or skin color, nationality, culture, or language. I'm referring to the universal church when I mention the body. I must admit, the more I study God's plan and program for the body, the more I believe in it, the more I admire what He has done and is doing, and the more I want to be involved.

When I meet folks who bad-mouth the church or see little significance in its existence, I pity that individual rather than feel offended. I realize he or she simply doesn't understand. It's a little like attending a symphony with someone who has no understanding of or appreciation for classical music. The whole event seems a waste of time and energy when, in actuality, the problem lies within his or her own mind.

Before I go any further, I should come up front and say that my desire in this book is to elevate your appreciation for the body of Christ, if by chance it's been sagging a little lately. In case you've gotten burned, had the edge of its significance dulled, or begun to question the necessity of your involvement in His projects, I want to come back to some basics and help you gain both a fresh perspective and a new appreciation.

It is no secret that I am a "satisfied customer" when it comes to the body. I am involved in it up to my ears. I'm not ashamed to confess that I think of it in the daytime, dream of it at night, and pour all of my creative energies into its mission and message. Because of my wholehearted belief, I seek to "sell the product" everywhere I go.

Ah, but be careful! Once this passion gets hold of you, you'll be addicted. Not only that, you'll realize that you haven't the time to be absorbed in the petty stuff so many superficial "churchy" folks focus on.

I notice that people who look upon the church as "a pretty good show for a nickel" spend a lot of time thinking about the clothing people wear, what kind of car they drive, how they look, the color of their skin, or the mess they've made of their former lives—horizontal issues, petty matters, small-picture stuff. Now *that's* a waste of time and energy! The longer I live and the better I understand the big picture, the less I even notice those petty things, . . . the less I care about horizontal hassles. That's not the church, that's man-made religion, designed to consume our energies and keep our vision out of focus.

Well, if that's not the church, then what is? We'll try to answer that question in the chapters that follow.

# Root Issues

1. Every local church body—if it is alive and animated by the Spirit of God—has a "cutting edge" . . . areas of the local community or world community where its impact for the Lord Jesus Christ is being felt and is making a difference. Where is your church's cutting edge? Are you part of the "action" . . . in the front lines of ministry? Through faithful, informed prayer? In a strategic support ministry? As you pray about your role in the King's Army, consider investing some focused conversation time on these issues with someone in your church's leadership.

2. Let the words of 1 Corinthians 15:58 sift down into the deepest part of your being as you draw encouragement and motivation for service from this marvelous promise.

3. Generations of popular "Wild West" novelists have created the image of the self-sufficient frontiersman . . . the squint-eyed, close-lipped, saddle-hardened, raw-boned fella who needs no one, trusts no one, and leans on no one (except maybe his horse). This mythology has penetrated every facet of American life . . . including the church. How does this go-it-alone mentality stack up against the truths expressed in 1 Corinthians 12? Read through that crucial chapter once again, asking the Holy Spirit to help you examine your own attitudes. Record your response in your notebook. This would be a good time to express in writing your commitment to the church.

4. When you hear that someone within your local church body is hurting because of a disappointment or loss, is your first thought, *What can I do to show my love and the love of Christ to that person?* or is it, *Well, someone else will surely do something—I don't even know him or her that well.* Let Romans 12:9-15, 1 John 4:7-12, and Philippians 2:4 guide you as you seek to become a wider, deeper channel for the love of our Lord within His body.

5. Are you helping your children learn faithfulness to the Lord and to His people through *giving*, perhaps by encouraging them to set aside a portion of their allowance for the Lord's work? How about considering a special "family project," perhaps selecting a missionary, "adopting" a Third World child, or assisting a struggling family in your community? Let the children feel the excitement and see the results as they learn to express the love of Christ through giving of their own means.

6. Have you ever felt "unprepared" for a time at the Lord's Supper? You felt, perhaps, like you had to do a quick "heart search" for unconfessed sin in your life. Or a "hurry-up" meditation on what the body and blood of our Lord really means to you in a personal way. While there is nothing wrong with either of these actions, you may find the time at the table to be a much more meaningful worship experience if you begin your heart preparation on *Saturday*. Before you slip between the covers that night, take a few minutes to ponder the familiar words of 1 Corinthians 11:21-31, or perhaps one of the "confession" psalms such as Psalm 32 or 51, or one of the Gospel accounts of that meal in the upper room or those dark hours on the cross. Ask your Lord to meet with you in a new way as you come to that simple meal.

 *Extending Your Roots*

This study focuses on the body of Christ—the church. Complete the following questionnaire about YOU and your involvement in God's worldwide construction projects.

1. Answer each part of the questionnaire with a word or check mark:

(1) At what age were you saved?

(2) Where did you make your profession of faith?

(3) Was your conversion: dramatic, traditional, out-of-focus, can't remember.

(4) Have you: ever doubted your salvation, never doubted, never think about it.

(5) Did you join the church *before* or *after* you were saved?

(6) Check a word describing your spiritual growth since salvation.

_____ roller-coaster

_____ gradual

_____ usually in times of crises

_____ no growth

_____ steady

(7) Do you faithfully have time alone with God?

(8) Is Christ part of your life-style?

(9) When the word *church* is mentioned, is your first mental image: a building, Sunday School, worship service, other.

(10) What is your pattern of participation at this time?

Outline a week's involvement.

Sunday

Monday

Tuesday

Wednesday

Thursday

Friday

Saturday

(11) Do you consider yourself part of a spiritual body involved in the mission and message of Christ?

(12) What does *your* church mean to you?

1. Many New Testament phrases or terms refer to the church. Using several translations, locate the Scripture where the following terms are used:

The body of Christ

The bride of Christ

A kingdom of priests

A fellowship

others . . .

2. What is your favorite term for "church"?

# 2 A Brief Historical Survey

Let's learn a little history together. Rather than listing numerous dates and dozens of people, I'll make this quick 'n easy. Ready?

The church in the first century—in its most pristine condition—was the object of God's attention and affection. It was purified by persecution, which caused its influence to spread like flames in a wheat field in Nebraska. Its contagious momentum impacted every little nook and cranny of the known world. People all across the Roman Empire, much to the embarrassment of its emperor, began to buy into it. And before long there were pockets of believers in villages, towns, and cities, none of them with ornate cathedrals you understand, but all of them with a heart for God. Their leaders walked with Jesus and taught His truth. Most of them ran the race until martyrdom. Many of their followers were handed the mantle and became the new leaders of the church. They, too, were martyred.

This fervent, often bloody chapter of history continued into the second, third, and fourth centuries. But during the latter part of that era, something strange happened in the body. Church became a formal thing. Christianity ultimately became an "official religion." It took upon itself the marks of an organization. Its leaders increased their roles of authority. Their authority finally shifted to unquestioned power, and soon there emerged *the* voice of *the* church. Worshipers, kept ignorant of the Word of God, became increasingly more manipulated and intimidated.

Predictably, the church lost its way as its divine power

was replaced with human authority. Zeal and excitement drained away. The shadow of the Dark Ages edged across the religious landscape. The church's authoritative guide—the Bible—was chained to the pulpit, with its message now hidden in the secret language of the clergy. Great edifices were built that pushed people away from the up-front leaders, holding them at bay. The common people remained in the dark—stone ignorant of the Scripture. It is hard to imagine the darkness of those decades. There were exceptions, but for the most part, God's truth was silenced. The church, like a bloated whale, lay awkward, enormous, *lifeless* atop the swells and waves of historic events. Its leaders existed in their private world—inaccessible and unaccountable.

That condition could endure only so long. By the fourteenth, fifteenth, and into the sixteenth century, a growing band of straight-thinking, tough-minded men emerged from obscurity. These "reformers" courageously stood against the uncontested power bloc of the official church and had the audacity to bring back the authority of Holy Scripture. As they broke with tradition, they spoke for God. Vital doctrines were rethought, restated, and reintroduced to the common people so that they could understand them and apply them to their lives. As you would expect, many of those reformers became martyrs, but their vision caught on. The fiery movement had gained too much momentum to be stopped. To the frowning dismay of the prelates of the church, these "protestants" became such a sizable body of people, they could no longer be swept aside and ignored. A spiritual revival swept across Europe and into England, igniting the Great Awakening that ultimately spanned the Atlantic to America.

The rest is familiar history. God's body-building program was again on the move. No power was strong enough to shut it down.

We have the Reformation to thank for the development of two major doctrines—*soteriology* (the doctrine of salvation) and *ecclesiology* (the doctrine of the church). The two are

*Growing Deep in the Christian Life: The Family of God*

inseparable, as we shall learn. I agree with theologian Lewis Sperry Chafer who said, "Next to salvation truth, it is vitally important for the believer to know the Bible doctrine of the Church."

## Extending Your Roots

Many people are surprised that what Jesus taught about the church is based on concepts from the Old Testament. Remember the word *covenant*? (Look up the word if you can't recall the meaning.)

1. Several covenants between God and people are listed below. Read God's covenant and identify the people.

Study the agreements and identify characteristics of God that are evident in churches today.

- Genesis 3:21-24
- Genesis 9:1-17
- Genesis 12:1-3; 15:18
- Exodus 19:5-6
- 2 Samuel 7:5-16; 1 Chronicles 17:4-14

## Taproot

On October 31, 1517, an Augustinian monk named Martin Luther nailed his Ninety-five Theses to the door of the Castle Church at Wittenberg. Things were never the same again for the body of Christ. The Reformation had begun.

Read a book about the Reformation or Martin Luther's life. Become informed about these tradition-breakers who chose to speak for God.

# 3 | Some Essentials About the Church

Down through the centuries, God's program has been like a massive crescendo mark on a musical score. From the church's beginning point on the day of Pentecost when the Spirit of God came (Acts 2), right up to the present day, it is ever expanding, ever enlarging. To represent its future growth we could add an extended dotted line, because the church, Christ's universal Body, will continue to enlarge. The church is larger today than it was yesterday. It will be larger tomorrow than it is today, because God is forever reaching people with the good news of Christ and bringing them into His Body.

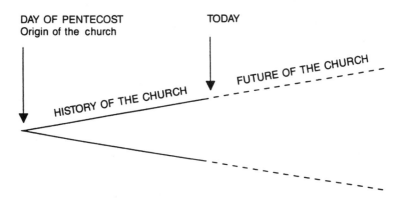

DAY OF PENTECOST
Origin of the church

TODAY

HISTORY OF THE CHURCH

FUTURE OF THE CHURCH

**Prediction**

Not only was the doctrine of the church developed late in history, even the mention of the term "church" appears late in Scripture—never once in the Old Testament and not until Christ is well underway in His ministry. Jesus mentions the church toward the end of a dialogue between Himself and His disciples. Matthew records the conversation in the sixteenth chapter:

> Now when Jesus came into the district of Caesarea Philippi, He began asking His disciples, saying, "Who do people say that the Son of Man is?" And they said, "Some say John the Baptist; some, Elijah; and others, Jeremiah, or one of the prophets." He said to them, "But who do you say that I am?" (vv. 13-15).

Jesus is asking that question to the whole group—the "you" is plural in verse 15. Now the reason I mention the plural "you" is because the whole group doesn't answer. Peter alone answers the question. We take a lot of shots at Peter, and he is often criticized for his weaknesses and failures; but the man stands tall at this moment. His answer is right on target!

> And Simon Peter answered and said, "Thou art the Christ, the Son of the living God" (v. 16).

Jesus offers a threefold response: first a blessing, then a promise, and finally a prediction.

> . . . Blessed are you, Simon Barjona, because flesh and blood did not reveal this to you, but My Father who is in heaven (v. 17).

"You've been talking with My Father, Peter—good for you! That came right from heaven. What insight!" That's the idea here. He continues:

> And I also say to you that you are Peter, and upon this rock I will build My church; and the gates of Hades shall not overpower it (v. 18).

Now look carefully at Jesus' promise, "I say to you that you are *Petros.*" My, that must have been wonderful for Peter to hear! We can't appreciate it, because we don't speak that language. Actually, Jesus gave him a nickname. All of his life Peter had been known as *Simon,* which, if you pressed it to the limit, would mean "vacillating one, shift-ing, moody, changing." But *Petros* meant "Rock." In effect, Christ says, "Good job, Rock. That's the way to go. That's the right answer. Peter, you're like a rock."

Then, drawing on that nickname, Jesus makes some promises "And upon this *Petra* . . ." *Petra* is not quite the same word as *Petros*. Some have taught that this means Jesus built His church on Peter. No, had that been the case, He would have said, ". . . upon this *Petros*—on you, Peter," but He didn't. Jesus built His Church on the rocklike truth Peter had just uttered. Matthew caught the significance by recording *Petra* "Upon this rocklike truth." And what is this truth? "You are the Messiah, the Anointed One, the Son of the Living God"—the very truth Peter had uttered when answering Jesus' opening question. And then Jesus predicted:

> . . . and upon this [truth] I will build My church; and the gates of Hades shall not overpower it (v. 18).

Stay with me for a minute while we snap on a telephoto lens and focus in closely on this crucial prediction: "I will build My church."

Note first to whom the church belongs—Jesus. "I will build *MY* church." It is not pressing the issue out of bounds to emphasize that the church is not the work of some pastor, priest, body of elders, or some other governing hierarchy. It is Jesus who builds it. The church is solely His. He doesn't have to clear His decisions with Rome, London, Wheaton, New York, or Minneapolis. The church is *not* owned by some denomination. Or group of clergymen. Or some official religious organization. Or the Pope himself.

To use today's terms, Christ is our Boss, our final author-ity. If I used a first-century term, Christ is our Lord, *Kurios,* and we are His servants; our *Despotes,* and we are His sub-jects. That has never changed, though in the passing of cen-turies all sorts of philosophies and governments have dictat-ed a different plan than that. The church was and is His genius. He originated it. He alone is its Master.

Let's zero in even closer. "I will *BUILD*." The dictionary says to *build* means "to form by uniting materials by gradual means into a composite whole, to construct." Another definition, "to develop by a definite process." That is going on right now in Christ's body. Always has been since the first century. His body-building program will never stop until Christ comes for His own. He's the Groom and He will come for His bride.

Sounds a little humorous to say it this way, but the bride is getting heavier every year, waiting for the Groom to come. She's enlarging her size. Every day she's getting bigger and bigger, waiting for His arrival. And the Groom will someday come and say to the bride, "You're mine. Come on home with Me." Until then He remains in the building process. And the building is made up of all nations, all cultures, all creeds, all languages, all colors. In fact, the church in the First World is fast becoming the minority as His body is being built up to an even greater degree in the Second and Third World countries.

Earlier we learned a little history, now let's learn a little Greek. This word *church* is translated from the Greek *ekklesia,* which comes from two words. The first is *ek,* a prefix particle meaning "out from among." The second is *klesia,* a derivative from the verb *kaleo,* "to call." Combining the two, *ekklesia* means "to call out from among." To render Jesus' prediction literally, "I will build My called-out ones."

What a wonderful thought! Since the beginning of the church, our Lord has been reaching down into the ranks of humanity, selecting, choosing, calling out, drawing people to Himself. These people are men, women, boys, girls, teenagers, older folks, all different sizes with all different personalities, from all different nations and tribes. He continues to "call them out" from the full spectrum of humanity, from busy urban centers to distant jungles. And He places them where? He places each one of them in His body. Because each one comes the same way, each one enjoys the same benefits.

Remember the little chorus:

I'm so glad I'm a part of the fam'ly of God—
I've been washed in the fountain, cleansed by His blood!
Joint heirs with Jesus as we travel this sod;
For I'm a part of the fam'ly, the fam'ly of God.[1]

Every one of us who is in the family of God can sing that because we've all come the same way. That means the body is exclusive—and I mean that in the right sense. The only way you become a member of this body is to place your total trust in Jesus Christ. This body is comprised of only believers in Christ. If you're a believer, you're in.

How permanent is it? Is it going to face the threat of extinction as time passes? We're back to the same Scripture for our answer. Christ said, "The gates of Hades shall not overpower it." In other words, if all the wicked forces were unleashed from the open gates of hell itself, the church would not be hindered in its growth. Nothing could ever destroy the church. It's a permanent building process that will never be crippled by some outside force, never be rendered obsolete, and never be stopped by any power, person, or plan. Period.

## Definition

Explanations are essential for clarification. There is nothing like a definition to pinpoint the meaning of terms. I suggest this definition for church: *The ever-enlarging body of born-again believers who comprise the universal body of Christ over whom He reigns as Lord.* I believe that covers all the essential bases. The Church is ever-enlarging, it is universal in scope, it is continually in process, it is exclusive in membership, and it is impervious to destruction.

Let me ask you: Can you think of anything more worthy of your time and treasure?

Not too many weeks ago, I had a moving conversation with an engineer who had recently decided to change his whole career in midstream. I'll bet you can guess why. He had gotten excited about God's world program. His decision was prompted by his local church. We had met at a conference where he shared his vision with me. He had made quite a decision regarding his future as he stepped away from the familiar into another realm.

"Why are you doing this?" I asked him.

"Well, Chuck," he said, "I'll be honest. I finally faced the fact that everything I was designing and building was some day going to wind up under a layer of dirt or ashes. Every project I was involved in had a termination point, while God's project is eternal. When that thought grabbed me, my whole mentality turned around."

Obviously, God does not lead everyone that way. He led the engineer that way when he got a fresh perspective of the church. When people begin to realize that church isn't just "a pretty good show for a nickel," but rather a passion for living with eternal dimensions, it revolutionizes their whole frame of reference. Their world suddenly enlarges from this tiny speck of time and circumstances to a worldwide, invincible project over which Christ serves as Lord.

## Extending Your Roots

1. The word *church* or *churches* appears 115 times in the New Testament. Read the following verses for interesting facts about the church. List your facts or discoveries beside each verse

Acts 19:32, 39, 41

Acts 7:38; Hebrews 2:12

Matthew 16:18

Ephesians 5:23, 25

1 Corinthians 1:2; 4:17

2. Using a hymnal, read "The Church's One Foundation." What key phrases or words are used to describe the church?

— *Taproot* —

1. Paul visited three local churches in Acts 14. Prepare a brief profile or description of each church. Locate the towns on a map.

Iconium                     Lystra                     Derbe

2. Later, Paul wrote a letter to these local churches. The letter is Galatians. Why?

3. Add additional information from this letter to your profile. What one message was Paul delivering to the local church?

Is the message the same today?

What process is involved in starting a local church?

# 4 Rapid Growth of the Early Church

Let's observe how rapidly the body expanded in its earliest years of existence. As the Holy Spirit came on the Day of Pentecost, He ignited a small body of people with enthusiasm and holy zeal. They poured out into the streets of Jerusalem and fearlessly declared their faith. "Petros" became their spokesman, and the immediate results were nothing short of phenomenal!

> So then, those who had received his word were baptized; and there were added that day about three thousand souls (Acts 2:41).

Think of it! Three thousand brand new believers. There they stood in the streets of Jerusalem. I love the thought of this!

They had no church building.

They had no pastor.

They had no "church constitution" (which is probably the reason they got along so well).

They had no board members . . . no handbook . . . no promise of what the future held for them.

Then what *did* they have? They had Christ! They had the unhindered, boundless joy of Christ's presence in their inner beings.

They also had each other. The ties of love held them closely together.

And what did they *do?*

> And they were continually devoting themselves to the
> apostles' teaching and to fellowship, to the breaking of bread
> and to prayer (v. 42).

They involved themselves in those four objectives—teaching, fellowship, the ordinances, and prayer. To this day those same four objectives are still the essentials of a church—teaching, fellowship, the ordinances (baptism, communion), and prayer.

Immediately this body of believers began to grow. The momentum grew as well.

> And at the hands of the apostles many signs and wonders
> were taking place among the people; and they were all with
> one accord in Solomon's portico. But none of the rest dared to
> associate with them; however, the people held them in high
> esteem. And all the more believers in the Lord, multitudes of
> men and women, were constantly added to their number
> (5:12-14).

Observe that the Lord kept His Word—He was building the body. That building process continued, in spite of hardship.

> And the word of God kept on spreading; and the number of
> the disciples continued to increase greatly in Jerusalem, and
> a great many of the priests were becoming obedient to the
> faith (6:7).

Look at that breakthrough. All these months the priests must have been wondering and thinking, *What's with these folks? Who are they? Why are they so happy, so confident, so closely connected to each other, so unintimidated?* Unable to ignore the movement, the priests became curious and began to listen. And then they got involved. And then, of all things, these formal, religious leaders tore away their masks of religion and committed their lives to the Lord Jesus Christ. Talk about revival!

Finally, because of persecution, the growth of the body extended beyond Jerusalem.

> So then those who were scattered because of the persecu-
> tion that arose in connection with Stephen made their way

to Phoenicia and Cyprus and Antioch, speaking the word to no one except to Jews alone. But there were some of them, men of Cyprus and Cyrene, who came to Antioch and began speaking to the Greeks also, preaching the Lord Jesus. And the hand of the Lord was with them, and a large number who believed turned to the Lord. And the news about them reached the ears of the church at Jerusalem, and they sent Barnabas off to Antioch. Then when he had come and witnessed the grace of God, he rejoiced and began to encourage them all with resolute heart to remain true to the Lord, for he was a good man, and full of the Holy Spirit and of faith. And considerable numbers were brought to the Lord (11:19-24).

We've seen televised pictures of volcanoes that have erupted, causing molten lava to pour over the lip of the crater and run down the crevices and on into the valley and villages below. Wherever the lava flows, it leaves its mark. I think of that when I think of those early years of the church. The heat of persecution drove the Christians into new regions, leading to further growth.

Just as Christ had predicted, the "gates of Hades" did not overpower the church. On the contrary, "considerable" numbers were "brought to the Lord." But the growth didn't stop there. It continued on into Greece and European regions. Lives were changed drastically as Christ's message penetrated and permeated. We see this clearly when we read of the events that transpired in Ephesus, a metropolitan center in western Turkey.

And this became known to all, both Jews and Greeks, who lived in Ephesus; and fear fell upon them all and the name of the Lord Jesus was being magnified. Many also of those who had believed kept coming, confessing and disclosing their practices. And many of those who practiced magic brought their books together and began burning them in the sight of all; and they counted up the price of them and found it fifty thousand pieces of silver. So the word of the Lord was growing mightily and prevailing (19:17-20).

What a remarkable account! How can it be that pagan

people could be changed so completely? Surely it involved more than simply "joining a church." Indeed! These changes occurred because Christ had invaded their lives. Let me explain that in the next chapter.

## *Extending Your Roots*

1. The early church is best described in Acts 2. Using a commentary, read about this chapter. On a map, locate the places mentioned in verses 9-11.

2. Prepare a brief outline of Peter's sermon (vv. 14-40). What invitation hymn would you choose for this occasion?

3. Verses 42-47 list activities of the early church. Read the verses in your translation and note the biblical phrase describing the activities.

Write the phrases or words below.

4. Compare your church to these activities.

5. Why do you think the "outsiders" were so eager to be a part of this fellowship of believers?

6. Would you like to have been a part of this early church? Explain.

## Taproot

As the first-century church grew, many characteristics became evident.

1. Read Acts 4:23-37. Focus on the idea of unity. Complete this statement: Spiritual unity in the church means:

2. Is spiritual unity lacking in your church?

3. How can you influence spiritual unity?

# 5 Changes that Occur When We Believe

When you trusted Christ Jesus as your Savior, many things happened to you. Two are crucial enough to mention.

1. Something happened *within* you. According to 2 Corinthians 5:17, you became an entirely new creation within.

> Therefore if any man is in Christ, he is a new creature; the old things passed away; behold, new things have come.

You gained new motivation, new interests. Your mind was no longer blinded to the truth of Scripture and held in bondage to fleshly lust. Your interests began to shift from yourself to others—from the things of the flesh to the things of God.

And a new group of people appeared on the horizon of your life—other Christians. You began to be more vulnerable, more open, more willing to confess the wrongs of your life. Your desire to hide from God changed to wanting to spend time with God. Why? You had become a new creature within.

2. Something happened *to* you. You were automatically and instantaneously placed into the family of God. You didn't necessarily feel any different. You didn't hear angelic choirs. You didn't see flashing lights or falling stars. But something happened to you the moment you believed. You became instantly related to God's forever family. And this new family relationship opened to you an entirely new realm you never before realized was in existence.

Those same two things happened to people in biblical

times. They became new creatures. They joined God's family. And those two factors never change!

# Extending Your Roots

One person in particular had a great influence on the early church. We might say, "He set a good example." Something wonderful had happened *within* him and *to* him.

1. Prepare a biographical study of Barnabas. Use a dictionary, reference Bible, and concordance for research.

These references will help you begin.
Acts 9:27 to 15:39
1 Corinthians 9:6
Galatians 2:1,9,13
Colossians 4:10

2. Not everyone could do what Barnabas did. However, several lessons from his example certainly apply to us and our church. Write two examples.

# Taproot

Two basic terms are used in the New Testament to describe the change that happens to us when we trust Jesus—"the indwelling of the Holy Spirit" and "the infilling of the Holy Spirit." Being Spirit-filled means having a changed life. We are still being changed.

1. How are you changed daily?

2. How are you changed devotionally?

3. What new discoveries have you made about yourself and your relationship to the body of Christ?

# 6 Vital Signs of a Healthy Church

Sometimes people ask, "Do I have to join a church to become a Christian?" My answer is, "No, but God always joins you to the church." No, you don't have to join some local church in order to become a Christian. He wants you to be connected with a local church, ultimately, but that's a separate issue from becoming a Christian. But you automatically become a member of the universal body, His church, when you believe. No problem there. But if we do encounter problems regarding the church, it will be when we cast our lot with a *local* church. It need not be an unhappy experience, but it often is. Why? Because the vital signs of health and wholeness are missing.

I remember when my mother died early in 1971, my father called me on the phone. He spoke very briefly and quietly as he told me that he thought my mom was dead.

"Sis is on her way," he said. "Can you come?"

Of course—I jumped into my car, and by the time I got there they had already covered my mother with a blanket as she lay lifeless on the sofa. She had died a very quick, painless death by heart attack.

As I arrived I said to my father and sister, "Have you called the doctor?"

"Well, no, we haven't," they replied. "We didn't really know what to do."

I grabbed the phone immediately and called her physician. He said, "Now, Charles, there are some vital signs you need to look for. Let's make absolutely certain—while the paramedics are on their way—that she is, in fact, dead." So he gave me four or five signs to check. We did exactly as he instructed us. They removed all doubt. The vital signs were missing. When the paramedics arrived, we stepped back and watched as they went through the same basic procedures. It was clear to all of us that she was gone.

When we think about a healthy body, the vital signs are important. I want to mention six vital signs of a healthy church. I find each one either mentioned or implied in 1 Corinthians 12.

First, *the presence of unity and harmony.*

> For even as the body is one and yet has many members, and all the members of the body, though they are many, are one body, so also is Christ (v. 12).

The first time I read that verse, it seemed like a tongue twister. Yet the longer I meditated on it, the clearer it became. It helps to change the word "member" to "organ," like the organs of the body. Let me do that for you, and you'll see how much clearer it reads:

> For even as the body is one and yet has many organs, and all the organs of the body, though they are many, are one body, so also is Christ's Body.

That's the idea here. The point I want you to see is the unity and harmony of the body. Though the church is comprised of many members, there is still only one body. Such unity is also emphasized in John 17:20-23 as well as Ephesians 4:1-6, which you should stop and read.

Second, another sign of good health is *the absence of favoritism, status, and prejudice.*

> For by one spirit we were all baptized into one body, whether Jews or Greeks, whether slaves or free, and we were all made to drink of one Spirit (v. 13).

In the first-century Roman world, the equality found in the church was much more significant than it is today. In that day there were definite castes (still familiar to the people of India, but not as much to the people of America). In those days there was nobility and there was slavery. There was the slave owner and the slave—nothing more than a human "tool" in the hands of his owner.

In another letter from Paul, these similar words appear:

> For you are all sons of God through faith in Christ Jesus. For all of you who were baptized into Christ have clothed yourselves with Christ. There is neither Jew nor Greek, there is neither slave nor free man, there is neither male nor female; for you are all one in Christ Jesus (Gal. 3:26-28).

In a healthy church one of the vital signs is an absence of favoritism, prejudice, and status. In any other earthly organization, when you draw together a number of human beings, you're going to have prejudice, emphasis on status, and a display of favoritism. But not in the body of Christ! This is one place that has no room for "preferred customers" or second-class citizens.

A third vital sign is *an emphasis on individual dignity and mutual variety.* We find this vital sign in 1 Corinthians 12:14-20. I love this passage. There's a little humor in it, so don't miss it. Think of the human body as you read these words.

> For the body is not one member, but many. If the foot should say, "Because I am not a hand, I am not a part of the body," it is not for this reason any the less a part of the body (vv. 14-15).

Feet can't go on strike. Because they are part of the body, the feet stay connected. It gets even more imaginative.

> And if the ear should say, "Because I am not an eye. I am not a part of the body," it is not for this reason any the less a part of the body (v. 16).

And now he carries the analogy to the ultimate extreme!

> If the whole body were an eye, where would the hearing be? If the whole were hearing, where would the sense of smell be? (v. 17).

Try to picture an "eye-body"—one massive six-foot eye! How useless, how unattractive. You couldn't hug it or kiss it. You wouldn't have anything to kiss with, unless you "batted each other" when you got up close. You'd get dirt in your eye all the time as you rolled around the house. You couldn't move around. Think of trying to drive a car or get into bed. The same could be said for an "ear-body." Bill Cosby could do wonders with verse 17, couldn't he?

By now you are smiling, and that's what you're supposed to do! The point is so ridiculous that it's humorous. We make six-foot eyeballs out of people. We make five-foot-nine-inch-ears out of certain people. We make them our stars, celebrities, big-time pedestal types. But they're just eyes and ears. They're just noses. They're just lips. No one person in the body is the whole body. Let's stop making idols out of people in the body! Sure, we need heroes, people we admire and love and respect. But we don't need six-foot eyeballs.

> But now God has placed the members, each one of them, in the body, just as He desired. And if they were all one member, where would the body be? But now there are many members, but one body (vv. 18-20).

Let's imagine this. You have just entered into God's family. God is speaking—

"Welcome to the family of God. I'm just passing out assignments. You . . . you'll be a nose. And that fella next to you . . . I'll make him a foot. Shorty over there, I'm going to make you something special. You'll be the big toe—part of the foot inside a sock inside a shoe. How does that sound?"

"Oh, rats!" Shorty replies. "Really had my heart set on being an eye. Hey, the foot already has enough parts. It doesn't need me."

Ever had a problem with some part of your foot? Maybe a tiny corn on your baby toe? A small callous? I know a lady who can hardly walk because of a minute growth on her foot. It needs attention, and the longer she waits, the more painful it becomes. Sometimes it hurts so much she has to sit down and lift her foot to get some relief. Even though a small growth on her smallest toe is the only problem, her whole body aches.

Ever tried to walk with a tiny pebble in your shoe? You can't stand it, so you take off your shoe and pull that baby outta there and find that it's really nothing but a speck of sand . . . but it felt like a boulder!

> But now God has placed the members, each one of them, in the body, just as He desired. And if they were all one member, where would the body be? But now there are many members, but one body (vv. 18-20).

Let's never forget this third vital sign: *an emphasis on individual dignity and mutual variety.*

Now we're ready for the fourth vital sign: *a de-emphasis on independence and self-sufficiency.* Listen to this, self-sufficient, strong and natural leaders! Pay attention, all entrepreneurs! Hear ye, hear ye, independent-minded Lone Rangers!

> And the eye cannot say to the hand, "I have no need of you"; or again the head to the feet, "I have no need of you." On the contrary, it is much truer that the members of the body which seem to be weaker are necessary; and those members of the body, which we deem less honorable, on these we bestow more abundant honor, and our unseemly members come to have more abundant seemliness (vv. 21-23).

Our younger daughter Colleen has a chronic problem with her pancreas. The tiny duct that secretes fluid is too tight to function properly. Every once in a while something will get lodged in that duct—perhaps a very small stone—and her whole body goes into an incredible spasm of pain. She's immobilized. You wouldn't think a pancreas would cause that big a deal. It's hard to believe that something that small could affect her whole body, but that's the way God made the body. No organ is completely independent and unrelated.

So it is in the body of Christ. There's a little member of the body down in there somewhere. And the happiness or sadness of the whole family of God rests on the functioning of that little, tiny part of the body. Interdependence cannot be ignored among the body members.

This brings us to the fifth vital sign: *the support of others, whether they are hurting or being honored.*

> that there should be no division in the body, but that the members should have the same care for one another. And if one member suffers, all the members suffer with it; if one member is honored, all the members rejoice with it (vv. 25*b*-26).

Isn't that great? Talk about a healthy church! Someone is hurting and you feel the sting of pain. Someone can't keep up; you slow down and encourage him or her. You are promoted and honored, others applaud and cheer. They rejoice as you rejoice. Is that the way it works? I hope so. What one member feels, all the others feel. That's the way it is to be in a healthy body.

Sixth and last: *exaltation of Christ as Head and supreme authority.*

> Now you are Christ's body, and individually members of it (v. 27).

Let us never forget that the body has one Head, only one. The Head, remember, is Christ. He—alone—is Lord.

Six characteristics identify a healthy church. Read the characteristics and think about the health of your church.

(1) Stewardship of time, money, and talents is more than adequate.
(2) Outreach and evangelism are consistently practiced.
(3) Leadership offers preaching, pastoring, and training.
(4) Sunday School is important.
(5) Worship services are worshipful.

(6) Members are involved.

1. On a scale from 1—5, rate your church.

| hospital | invalid | see doctor | good/bad days | healthy |
|:---:|:---:|:---:|:---:|:---:|
| 1 | 2 | 3 | 4 | 5 |

2. Based on your rating, write a prescription for your church.

Several healthy and sick churches are mentioned in the New Testament. Using a concordance, read about each church and give your "professional" diagnosis. You may also want to write a prescription.

1. Antioch

2. Ephesus

3. Jerusalem

4. Corinth

5. Smyrna


6. Pergamum


7. Thyatira


8. Sardis


9. Philadelphia


10. Laodicea

# 7 Diseases that Cripple the Church

Staying with the same analogy of the human body, there are some diseases that can spread infection throughout the body. The mind can become swollen with pride. The heart can grow cold and indifferent because of sin. The digestive system can get clogged by sterile theory and unapplied theology, so the body can't digest what needs to be turned into energy or eliminate what needs to be released. When that occurs we start to fight among ourselves or we lose our equilibrium and find ourselves unable to stay balanced.

Let me get even more specific: The body can have eyes that feed on lust and greed, tongues that wag, and ears that listen to gossip. (I don't know of any disease that's hurting the body worse these days than a wagging, unrestrained tongue.) It can have knees that seldom bend to the lordship of Christ; hands that applaud the works of man more than the work of God; minds that are closed to new ideas; emotions that are either out of control or under rigid wraps; muscles that are not exercised—mental muscles that have stopped being stretched, financial muscles that have stopped releasing with generosity, faith muscles that have become soft and flabby.

Where are you in that physical analysis of the church? What's your temperature? How's your health? Is it possible that your condition is more serious than you may suspect? A Christian physician challenges our thinking with his penetrating words.

Sometimes a dreaded thing occurs in the body—a mutiny—resulting in a tumor. . . .

A tumor is called benign if its effect is fairly localized and it stays within membrane boundaries. But the most traumatizing condition in the body occurs when disloyal cells defy inhibition. They multiply without any checks on growth, spreading rapidly throughout the body, choking out normal cells. White cells, armed against foreign invaders, will not attack the body's own mutinous cells. Physicians fear no other malfunction more deeply: it is called cancer. For still mysterious reasons, these cells—and they may be cells from the brain, liver, kidney, bone, blood, skin, or other tissues—grow wild, out of control. Each is a healthy, functioning cell, but disloyal, no longer acting in regard for the rest of the body.

Even the white cells, the dependable palace guard, can destroy the body through rebellion. Sometimes they recklessly reproduce, clogging the bloodstream, overloading the lymph system, strangling the body's normal functions—such is leukemia.

Because I am a surgeon and not a prophet, I tremble to make the analogy between cancer in the physical body and mutiny in the spiritual body of Christ. But I must. In His warnings to the church, Jesus Christ showed no concern about the shocks and bruises His Body would meet from external forces. "The gates of hell shall not prevail against my church," He said flatly (Matthew 16:18). He moved easily, unthreatened, among sinners and criminals. But He cried out against the kind of disloyalty that comes from within.[1]

Few doctrines are more important than this one. Because the church is under constant attack, we need to be good students of the subject. Because we are fellow members of the body, we need to apply ourselves to mutual harmony. And because disease can diminish the effectiveness of the body, we must maintain habits of health and a consistent program of exercise in harmony with God's body-building program.

Furthermore, a regular checkup by the Great Physician is a must. Not once a year but at least once a week. And be prepared for the cost of that visit.

If you're looking to get it done for a nickel, you're in for a real surprise.

## Extending Your Roots

Wouldn't it be nice if shots or vaccines were available for sick churches? Or spiritual vitamins were distributed regularly to the body of Christ as a preventive measure?

1. Listed below are some possible disease-causing actions. Determine how these actions can cripple a church. Write your diagnosis.

- neglect in teaching doctrines
- no emphasis on mission giving or offerings
- no life-application from the Bible
- meaningless Lord's Supper
- no planned churchwide fellowships
- no effectual, fervent praying
- no praise or too much praise
- no burden for unsaved people
- lack of interest in social issues.

2. Do you think your church has the potential for a crippling disease?

## Taproot

1. Select a familiar hymn tune and write new lyrics based on this chapter—the body of Christ. Read or sing your song about the church.

# 8 Three Cheers for the Church

You remember Alexander, don't you? Well, maybe not. I introduced him to many of my readers a few years ago. Some of you may have forgotten. The little book that contained a slice out of his day was called *Alexander and the Terrible, Horrible, No Good, Very Bad Day*. This kid is my kind of guy. The stuff he goes through is so typical, you'd swear you've been inside his skin.

I'm glad to say that the lady who wrote his biography (I think it was his mother, Judith Viorst) has continued to write. She's written a book about herself called *How I Became Forty . . . and Other Atrocities*. Great little book!

Then she wrote *If I Were in Charge of the World and Other Worries*, which is pretty close to something that Alexander might have written. So think about that little five- or six-year-old fellow when you read the next few lines:

> If I were in charge of the world
> I'd cancel oatmeal,
> Monday mornings,
> Allergy shots.
>
> If I were in charge of the world
> There'd be brighter night lights,
> Healthier hamsters, and
> Basketball baskets forty-eight inches lower.
>
> If I were in charge of the world
> You wouldn't have lonely.
> You wouldn't have clean.

You wouldn't have bedtimes.
Or "Don't punch your sister."
You wouldn't even have sisters.

If I were in charge of the world
A chocolate sundae with whipped cream and nuts
would be a vegetable.

All 007 movies would be G.
And a person who sometimes forgot to brush,
And sometimes forgot to flush,
Would still be allowed to be
In charge of the world.[1]

Like I said, he's my kind of guy. Actually, I've been thinking about that line for a long time: "If I were in charge of the world . . . ." If that were ever true, what would I do?

If God allowed me to be in charge for just twenty-four hours, I'd do *one* thing . . . *I'd change people's opinion about the church.* I would remove all prejudice about the church. I would erase all church scars and heal all church splits, all church bruises, and all hurts that came from church gossip. I would remove all those horrible offenses. And in place of all that? I would have everybody see only the value of the church. If all I had was twenty-four hours, that's what I'd do if I were in charge of the world.

But since I'm not, I will ask you to do the next best thing: I will ask you to take charge of your thoughts. And for the next few pages I challenge you to allow no negative thoughts about the church to enter your mind, only positive ones. (No fair cheating, now.) I'll do that with you. And let's see what a marvelous thing God has done in giving us churches.

Negative thoughts and opinions prevent a believer from

seeing what a marvelous thing God has done in giving us churches.

1. Evaluate your thoughts and opinions about your church by responding "yes" or "no" to these statements.

_____ The way people dress at church bothers me.

_____ I enjoy our worship music.

_____ Children should sit with their parents.

_____ The pastor preaches a subject to death.

_____ The prayers are too long.

_____ A longer invitation (altar call) is needed.

_____ We spend too much time in the New Testament.

_____ People have a right to their favorite pew.

2. If the apostle Paul were writing about your church, would he repeat 2 Thessalonians 1:3-4?

## Taproot

Faith, visible in the body of Christ, is evidence of maturity. The author of Hebrews helps us understand this concept. The writer gives many examples of those who have demonstrated faith. (See Heb. 10:19 to 13:26.) The author also talks about the church.

1. The following verses are called the *let us* verses. Read each verse and record what the body of Christ is to do.

Hebrews 10

v. 22_____

v. 23_____

v. 24_____

v. 25_____

v. 25
Hebrews 12
v. 1_____
v. 2_____

2. Can your church be recognized as a maturing body of Christ?

# 9 For a Few Minutes, Remember Some Churches

Let's go back to our childhood. Let's go way back. Let's go all the way back to when we first heard the hymns and we first listened to sermons and we first formed our impressions about church. And while we do that, let's allow the Letter to the Philippians to guide us in our mental journey.

## Days of Childhood

Some of us have very pleasant memories. A few, unfortunately, are not so pleasant. But since we're committed to staying on the sunny side of the street for a few pages, we may need to think of the kind of church we would have wanted to have as a child if we can't think of one that was real. For some, it was an urban church located in a busy city. And there were cars buzzing by outside and horns honking because of busy intersections. And there were multiple buildings and wide hallways and stained-glass windows. Maybe when you were a little child, you were in a big, Gothic-style church. Others were raised in a suburban church—the distant city just visible on the skyline. Perhaps your home was within walking distance. For many of us, it was a country church with a steeple, located in a rural part of the state where we lived—like the one William Pitts wrote of years ago:

> There's a church in the valley by the wildwood,
> No lovelier place in the dale;
> No spot is so dear to my childhood
> As the little brown church in the vale.

> Oh, come to the church in the wildwood,
> Oh, come to the church in the dale.
> No spot is so dear to my childhood
> As the little brown church in the vale.[1]

That was my church: little country town, little country church. But what a place! To this day I cherish healthy memories about that little house of worship.

> Paul and Timothy, bond-servants of Christ Jesus, to all the saints in Christ Jesus who are in Philippi, including the overseers and deacons: I thank my God in all my remembrance of you, always offering prayer with joy in my every prayer for you all, in view of your participation in the gospel from the first day until now (Phil.1:1, 3-5).

A statement in verse 3 should be linked with a thought in verse 5: "I thank my God in all my remembrance . . . in view of your participation in the gospel from the first day . . . ."

Think about your "first church." You were just a little girl or you were just a little guy. It was probably there where you first received formal instruction and learned to respect the authority of Scripture. You learned to sit still (longer than you wanted) and to pay attention to something you didn't fully understand. You remember those early days when you listened to the hymns, when you formed your earliest religious impressions. It was there you discovered that there were people who believed in God with all their heart. You probably sang your first solo there. Saw your first wedding, funeral, and baptism. Joined your first choir or ensemble. It was there you discovered that you had leadership skills. It was there you learned the hard way that when God speaks it's best to listen, and not only listen, but also to obey.

It was there you gave yourself to that first group of people. They became a part of your life. You saw them every week, and you laughed with them, you wept with them, you celebrated with them, and you grieved with them. Just a little pocket of people. And because of them, the seasons had new meaning. Easter, Thanksgiving, and Christmas took on new color—even the new year gained purpose and significance. You thank God upon every remembrance of those people who were partners with you in the gospel. You and I have the church to thank for all those rich childhood memories.

## Times of Crisis

Now let's travel a little deeper into the time tunnel and recall times of crisis in our past.

> For it is only right for me to feel this way about you all, because I have you in my heart, since both in my imprisonment and in the defense and confirmation of the gospel, you all are partakers of grace with me. For God is my witness, how I long for you all with the affection of Christ Jesus (vv. 7-8).

Observe his reference to imprisonment. Let's let that represent our trials, our life crises. Think about that. You may have lost your mom or your dad or a brother or sister. And as helpful as the hospital staff or the physician tried to be, no one could minister to you like the people of the church. No one put their arms around you and said "I understand" like they did.

Some of you can recall stumbling out of the physician's office, having heard the news about the disease that could (and probably *would!*) take your life. It most likely was not a neighbor or some coworker at the office who entered into your crisis and said. "I understand"; it was someone at your church.

When your mate said, "It's over, I'm leaving," and then walked out, who helped you cope? In all of the embarrassment, the rejection, the anger, and the disillusionment, you probably didn't receive comfort from someone at the local bar or your bridge club. Chances are good that there was somebody from your church who said, "I've got a scar like that. And while you're hurting, I want you to know that I hurt with you. Even though you feel pushed out of society and shoved aside like a second-class bum, I understand your pain. And I stand in defense of you. In fact I love you."

Remember when grief struck you at the deepest level? Remember when your loved one was put in a casket? Maybe the banker could tell you where you could find a loan to get you through that hard time. Or maybe the insurance man helped you by bringing the check. Perhaps an attorney gave you sound advice. But who was there when the flowers wilted? Chances are good, the person who spoke well of your departed loved one was the pastor of a church. The people who surrounded you and gave you hope to go on were church people. They understood your world, they brought light to your darkness. That's the way God designed the church.

Remember disillusionment as a youth? (Just spend a moment thinking about that! I've never met anybody who wanted to be a teenager again.) Crisis after crisis. And remember the youth pastor who believed in you when you didn't even believe in yourself? Remember the Sunday School teacher who said she (or he) loved you, *regardless?*

Remember not knowing exactly what you should do in your career, and some pastor spoke directly from the Scripture, cutting a clear path of purpose through your dense fog of confusion?

Remember the tape of some sermon you played over and over and over again? What if there had never been a church? What if there had never been a cassette recording of some pastor who ministered to you? Remember, it wasn't from some law office or from some doctor's waiting room or even from some funeral home that your help came. Quite likely, your help to go on came from the church.

## Extending Your Roots

Some people spend their whole life going to one church. They "grew up in the church." Other people have been members of many churches in many places.

1. Recall your earliest memories about church. Jot down a few.

2. Now, think of a church that made a great impact on your life. Like the apostle Paul so often did, write a letter to that body of Christ and express your feelings.

Dear _____ Church,

Greetings. Do you remember me? My name is _____. I want to tell you

Sincerely,

If your memories are not happy ones, write a letter expressing your hurts. Paul did that too!

Paul, a prisoner in Rome, wrote a joyful letter to the church in Philippi. To become acquainted with this church, read Acts 16:11-40.

1. Study the Letter to the Philippians. Notice ways to be joyful in suffering, serving, believing, and giving. Apply these four words to churches from your past.

2. Record your experiences in suffering or crisis and how the body of Christ helped you.

3. List ways you have served in churches.

4. Through the teaching of churches, what have you come to believe about the New Testament church?

5. Is your giving today of time, talent, and money a result of past teachings or worship? Explain.

# 10 Moments of Celebration

While we're traveling memory's lane, let's not miss the flowers!

> And this I pray, that your love may abound still more and more in real knowledge and all discernment, so that you may approve the things that are excellent, in order to be sincere and blameless until the day of Christ; having been filled with the fruit of righteousness which comes through Jesus Christ, to the glory and praise of God (vv. 9-11).

Where did you find your mate? More than likely you (like I) found her or him in a church. Where were you married? If you weren't married in a church, you probably wish you could have been. Who gave you the best counsel? Probably a pastor. Who was there to dedicate your first baby? Who said, "Marriage gets a little cold. And we've got a conference designed to help add a little spark to it"? Who ministered to you when you really got scared about how to rear your family? Who said, "We affirm the family. We stand with you all the way through it, even at this time when your daughter has run away. We're here. We're not leaving"? Who was most effective in convincing her not to get an abortion? Who rejoiced with you when she turned back to the Lord?

Celebration times. Times of praise. Times when we are

> filled with the fruit of righteousness which comes through Jesus Christ, to the glory and praise of God (v. 11).

How about when you made a decision to serve the Lord

Jesus in your future career? How about when you celebrated a graduation out of school, and maybe even out of seminary? Who was there to say, "We're with you, we applaud your achievement—and if God leads you overseas, we won't forget you"? Perhaps the church held you closer than your own family. Perhaps the church contributed more to your income than any family member has ever contributed, because the church believed in you.

When a pastor, a music minister, or an associate pastor defects from the faith, the tragedy will make the headlines. How often a church split will scandalize a neighborhood . . . or a brother or sister become offensive and say an ugly thing to you, or about you. And that weighs on your mind so heavily it possesses your thinking when someone brings up the subject of church. I know many people today who say, "Don't bother me with church. I've had it up to here." I understand. But I am saddened to meet people so jaded because I realize how much they lose. There will come a day when those same bitter people will need the church. What a marvelous thing is the local family of God!

Let me go a step further. As helpful and beneficial as most parachurch ministries are, they are all dependent upon the church to exist. When you're in college and Inter-Varsity, Campus Crusade, or some other campus ministry has really guided you and encouraged you, it is worth singing praises to God. But when you graduate, you need a church. The church, alone, has staying power.

It is in the church, week after week, where we learn faithfulness. It is in the church that we first learn to give and to tithe. It was the first place I gave out of my allowance. I remember squeezing my allowance in my hot little hand until I thought the buffalo would roar. But my mom and dad convinced me, "Son, this is where part of your money goes." It is in the church that we first learn generosity. I didn't give it to a friend. I didn't give it to a family member. Or a school. I gave it to God's work. It is in the church that discipleship is carried out. It is in the church that accountability is modeled. It is in the church that marriage is upheld and singleness is dignified without your being hustled. It is in the church of Jesus Christ that we find the doctrinal roots that establish us in our faith.

When the plan to reach out onto some foreign soil is determined, the church is there to make it happen. When an evangelistic series is promoted in the community, it is the church that does so. When the project is over, when the crusade team members have all gone home, *the church stays*. It takes the new converts and nurtures them into their own walk. Three cheers for the church! In spite of all her weaknesses and human flaws, it is still the most significant rallying point for Christians on this earth today. It will continue to be so until Jesus Christ returns.

 *Extending Your Roots*

1. When people make a statement like this, "I grew up in my church," what do they mean? If you can make this statement, what do you mean? What caused you to grow?

2. Recall times when the church helped you grow or make a major decision as a:

CHILD

TEEN

SINGLE ADULT


PARENT


SENIOR ADULT


3. Complete this statement: I thank God for my church because


## *Taproot*

Imagine that you are the editor of *The Jerusalem Journal*. The feature front-page article is about a new kind of meeting going on in the city. The focus is on a group of people called disciples.

1. Develop the front-page format. Include articles about what the church is celebrating. Include an editorial. Most of your research will come from the Book of Acts and a concordance.

# 11 Why the Church Is So Significant

Let me show you why the church is significant in the world and in the community.

## In the World

> Now I want you to know, brethren, that my circumstances have turned out for the greater progress of the gospel, so that my imprisonment in the cause of Christ has become well-known throughout the whole praetorian guard and to everyone else, and that most of the brethren, trusting in the Lord because of my imprisonment, have far more courage to speak the word of God without fear (vv. 12-14).

I understand that Paul means this personally. But allow me to broaden the application and apply it to the church. Why is the church significant to the world? Because the church represents penetrating light and undiluted salt in a lost, confused, insipid society. Interestingly, when a church remains neutral on a moral issue that affects the community, the public will criticize that church. The public will state that the church has let the community down. In the public arena, the church of Jesus Christ is *expected* to stand for righteousness. Even the uncommitted, the nonchurch crowd know in their hearts that a church that is weak regarding sin has lost its way.

I remember reading about the late President Calvin Coolidge, who returned home from attending church early one Sunday afternoon. He was asked by his wife what the minister spoke on.

"Sin," Coolidge replied.

Wanting to know more, she pressed for some words of explanation. And being a man of few words with his wife, he responded, "I think he was against it."

When the pulpit denounces sin, people are influenced to stand against it. When the pulpit speaks on moral issues, people learn to penetrate the fog of compromise and gain courage to stand alone. For many, many years in our nation the church gave our nation its conscience. As its pulpits stood, its people stood.

"You are the salt of the earth," said Jesus. "You are the light on a hill. Don't put a bushel basket over it." Let the light shine. Let the salt bite. That's your role, Christian! The world expects it from us, even though it doesn't agree. In Paul's day "the whole praetorian guard" became aware of Christ! Even though many will not enter the doors of a local church (though they are invited), they expect us to stand for the truth as we see it in the Scripture. To do less is to diminish our distinctives and to lose our integrity.

## In the Community

Are you ready for a surprise? What I am about to write will make a few of my readers swallow hard. Some of you who look with a squint-eye at other ministries, criticizing them because they don't agree with you, are going to be shocked by these next four verses:

> Some, to be sure, are preaching Christ . . . out of selfish ambition, rather than from pure motives, thinking to cause me distress in my imprisonment. What then? Only that in every way, whether in pretense or in truth, Christ is proclaimed; and in this I rejoice, yes, and I will rejoice (vv. 15,17-18).

Why is the church significant in the community? For at least two reasons. First of all, because churches provide the availability of variety. And second, because churches offer a singularity of message. Here's what this passage is saying. There will be churches of all different kinds. Think of the

windshield wiper on your car. Churches will go from one extreme to another. Churches that are worth attending and
supporting have the same pivot point, the Lord Jesus
Christ. Christ is exalted. Christ is declared. Christ is central.
But some will go at it from one direction, while others will
go at it from another. A different style of worship. Another
approach, emphasis, and methodology. And even a difference in *motive* (according to what Paul wrote).

J. B. Phillips translates these verses:

> I know that some are preaching Christ out of jealousy, in
> order to annoy me, but some are preaching him in good faith.
> These latter are preaching out of their love for me. For they
> know that I am here in prison to defend the gospel. The mo-
> tive of the former is questionable—they preach in a partisan
> spirit, hoping to make my chains even more galling than
> they were. But what does it matter? However they may look
> at it, the fact remains that Christ is being preached, whether
> sincerely or not, and that fact makes me very happy
> (vv. 15-18).

I have a strong word to all who are given to public criti-
cism of other ministries. Watch yourself! Rather than being
discerning, you may have become too narrow and rigid!
Learn from Paul. Even ministries that may employ a few
deceptive motives, even churches that you choose not to attend, Paul said, in effect, "I rejoice that at least Christ is
proclaimed."

Let's face it, if everybody attended where you attend, the
community couldn't fit in. We must learn to give God praise
that there is a variety of ministries. We gain nothing by promoting the idea that we have *the* corner on the truth, and
that our pastor is the only one who has *the* answers for life.
No, no, a thousand times, no! God may be using this person-
with his style for this ministry and that person with another
approach for that ministry—each one exalting and present-
ing Christ to different types of people.

My advice? Don't waste your time criticizing other ministries. Just attend the one that you prefer and give God
praise that Christ is exalted. You may be thinking, *Sounds*

*pretty liberal to me.* Well, it sounds biblical to me. If Philippians 1:15-20 isn't teaching that, then, frankly, I'm at a loss to know what it means. In our zeal it is very easy to think we've got the *only* church with the *only* answers for the entire community. We don't.

As a pastor, I am relieved and grateful that I am not the only fish in the pond. What an awesome responsibility that would be! Furthermore, that's *Christ's* role, since He is the Head of the church. I look back on some of the things I have said, and I realize now I gave wrong counsel—or weak, at best. On occasion I listen to some of the cassette-taped sermons I once preached (which is always a tough assignment!), and I no more agree today with what I said back then than the man in the moon! After a few years I see it in a little different light and my words come back to haunt me. I'm so grateful not everybody believed my stuff way back then any more than they do now!

And while I'm confessing, I might as well admit, I'm thankful that even when I preached with the wrong motive (as I have on a few occasions, much to my shame), God honored His message at that time and rebuked me later. You see, in many communities there is a variety of churches available, but, praise God, if you listen attentively, you're going to hear Christ preached. Stop exalting one church as though it were *the only* place to attend! It is not. We would do well to remember that Christ is to be exalted—not some church.

Since the late 1970s God has allowed my wife and me to serve together in a radio ministry, "Insight for Living." She directs the operation of this outreach (with the help of almost one hundred and fifty others) as I supply the voice and the messages. To our continual surprise, the Lord has given growth and caused His name to be increasingly more exalted through these broadcasts. Occasionally, I have wondered why. Perhaps one of the reasons is that we have no interest whatsoever in either promoting ourselves or in criticizing others. God's hand is on *many* ministries, and He is using *many* ministers to get the job done. They differ from us in style, often in content, and perhaps in objective or even motive. But those who are proclaiming Christ cause us to rejoice. After all, they are able to reach certain folks we would never reach.

The same could be said of the church I pastor. There are many churches in southern California. They range in variety from the superconservative to the loosey-goosey extreme. But the interesting fact is this: People attend every one of them. They choose to go there because they are ministered to and because they are comfortable with the style, the approach, the objectives. For every place where Christ is proclaimed and exalted, I sincerely rejoice. Thank God, I'm not the jealous or the competitive type. If God raised up those ministries, who am I to tear them down? That would not only be disobedient, it would be a waste of precious time and energy.

### For the Christian

The church is significant not only to the world and in the community but to the Christian as well.

> But I am hard-pressed from both directions, having the desire to depart and be with Christ, for that is very much better; yet to remain on in the flesh is more necessary for your sake. And convinced of this, I know that I shall remain and continue with you all for your progress and joy in the faith, so that your proud confidence in me may abound in Christ Jesus through my coming to you again. Only conduct yourselves in a manner worthy of the gospel of Christ; so that whether I come and see you or remain absent, I may hear of you that you are standing firm in one spirit, with one mind striving together for the faith of the gospel; in no way alarmed by your opponents—which is a sign of destruction for them, but of salvation for you, and that too, from God. For to you it has been granted for Christ's sake, not only to believe in Him, but also to suffer for His sake, experiencing the same conflict which you saw in me, and now hear to be in me (vv. 23-30).

This passage tells us something that the Masonic Lodge or

the bowling team will never tell us. It says something the school board or the city council will never tell us. The church alone tells the Christian to:

> conduct yourselves in a manner worth of the gospel of Christ.

You won't hear that from any other organization! No one will push hard against your breastbone and say, "Shape up your life. Get with it. You say you're a Christian? Walk like it. You've done wrong? Confess it and come back to God."

No one else does that. Only the church.

I'll add more—only those who continue faithfully in the attendance of church services will hear reproof, exhortation, encouragement, and rebuke that will help keep their lives in line. In fact, I recently came up with a list of four specific benefits of church attendance:

- Accountability
- Consistency
- Unity
- Stability

I won't take the time to develop each one, but they are interwoven through these verses.

What I have observed is that Christians who lose faith in a local church and walk away, saying, "No thanks, I don't need it," have struggles, without exception, in one or more of these four areas—sometimes all four. They lose (or *wish* to lose) accountability. They lack consistency in their walk. They cultivate an independent spirit, rather than an interdependence of love and concern. And when pressure strikes, they lack stability. Why? The answer isn't that complicated: There's no family around.

My counsel is predictable—before you think that you really don't need a church, run down that list one more time. The consequences are inescapable. Especially if you have available to you a small group of caring, loving folks with whom you are free to interact, share the details of your life, and enter into theirs as well.

I might also add that apart from the church, there is no

place to observe the sacred ordinances— something I dare not overlook in this book on doctrine.

## Extending Your Roots

1. Why is the church significant to the community and to the world? Write *your* answer below.

2. The following references focus on the word *salt*. Read each verse and determine how or why the Bible wants us to be salt shakers.

Leviticus 2:13

Matthew 5:13

Mark 9:50

Luke 14:34-35

3. A salty church is significant to the community and the world. On a scale of one to ten, with ten being highest:

How salty are you?             How salty is your church?

1. Pretend you are a parent of a church-going family. Regular attendance is important to you. Your teenage son has started asking, "Why do we have to go to church all the time?" You normally reply, "Just because." Today however, you have called a family meeting. The agenda is set. The subject is "Why going to church faithfully is significant in this family."

Prepare your explanation below:

# 12 Two Ordinances Unique to the Church

In this wonderful body called the church, God has given two very unique sacraments or celebrations. In no other organization will you find such things. One is called the Lord's Supper (your church may call it Communion, the Eucharist, or simply the table). The other is baptism. The Lord's Supper is a memorial of remembrance, and baptism is a celebration of reflection. With no desire to offend anyone, I sometimes think of them as sacred pantomimes. They are sermons without words, full of symbolic significance. The Lord's Supper is saying, "He died for me." The baptismal celebration is saying, "He lives in me."

Both require only a few words of explanation. Both are for believers only. Both are rich in symbolism, yet beautiful in simplicity. And both make bold statements to the world regarding the Christian faith.

Neither, however, is essential for salvation. By that I mean that they are *because of* salvation, not a means to it. Yet neither is to be treated lightly or viewed as if they are of little importance.

## The Lord's Supper

Have you stopped lately to think about the Lord's Supper? What a simple ceremony—and so strange in the eyes of the world! A little bit of pastry and a swallow of liquid—how strange. In places all around the world there are little pieces of pastry and there are little cups of wine or juice. Regardless of the exact substance, or the amount, it is what each represents that is so extremely important—the bread representing our Savior's body and the cup representing His blood, both given for us at the cross. Both, taken in His remembrance, cause us to recall that He died for us.

I've often stated publicly that one of the most memorable communion times I can remember takes me back to the early 1960s when I was with a large group of Christian collegians up on the northern California coastline, not far from Santa Cruz. It was a church-sponsored outing. We were sitting on a windswept, chilly beach. We had sung a few songs around sunset. All we had to serve were chips and cola. Yet it was marvelous! I have never before or since served chips and cola at the Lord's Supper, but the elements were insignificant. Our Lord's presence was there in the sunset over the Pacific, in the pounding of the surf, in the faces of those young believers, in the tears that fell, in the testimonies that were spoken. And we worshiped our God as we met at that open place, sand between our toes, swimming suits on, towels wrapped around us as we shivered around the fire and passed the chips and cola among us. We did it all "in remembrance of Me."

The biblical basis for the Lord's Supper takes us back to the last meal Jesus had with His disciples before He was crucified. Matthew records the event in the simplest of terms.

> And while they were eating, Jesus took some bread, and after a blessing, He broke it and gave it to the disciples, and said, "Take, eat; this is My body." And when He had taken a cup and given thanks, He gave it to them, saying, "Drink from it, all of you; for this is My blood of the covenant, which is poured out for many for forgiveness of sins. But I say to you, I will not drink of this fruit of the vine from now on until that day when I drink it new with you in My Father's kingdom." And after singing a hymn, they went out to the Mount of Olives (Matt. 26:26-30).

The apostle Paul draws upon the scene when he later writes these words in the First Corinthian Letter:

> For I received from the Lord that which I also delivered to you, that the Lord Jesus in the night in which He was betrayed took bread; and when He had given thanks, He broke it, and said, "This is My body, which is for you; do this in remembrance of Me" (1 Cor. 11:23-24).

Obviously, participation is not optional; on the contrary, it is a command, "Do this . . . !" Don't look upon the Lord's Supper simply as an available, optional part of your worship. We are assigned by God to do it continually. In fact, the command is a present imperative, "Keep on doing this in remembrance of Me."

Some observe the Supper every time they meet. Some observe it every other week. Some "keep on doing this" once a month. To me it would seem inappropriate to observe it less frequently than once a month since we are to "keep on doing this."

The instruction continues:

> In the same way He took the cup also, after supper, saying, "This cup is the new covenant in My blood; do this, as often as you drink it, in remembrance of Me." For as often as you eat this bread and drink the cup, you proclaim the Lord's death until He comes (vv. 25-26).

We'll be eating together at this simple table in our churches until our Savior returns. It will be regularly observed by believers in rugged churches with thatched roofs, as well as in beautiful cathedrals with high ceilings and ornate wall lined by stained glass—in brand-new places of worship only a week or two old, as well as in places centuries old, they'll still be observing the Lord's Supper. That's the church ordinance.

The place is not significant, but the condition of the heart is. Before we ever eat the bread or drink from that cup, each Christian asks within himself, "Is there anything between my Father and me? Is my heart clean?" A strong warning is attached to the instruction:

> Therefore whoever eats the bread or drinks the cup of the Lord in an unworthy manner, shall be guilty of the body and

the blood of the Lord. But let a man examine himself, and so let him eat of the bread and drink of the cup. For he who eats and drinks, eats and drinks judgment to himself, if he does not judge the body rightly. For this reason many among you are weak and sick, and a number sleep (vv. 27-30).

The Corinthians turned the Lord's Supper into a carnal event. Instead of an atmosphere of worship and humble confession, they made light of the event by eating too much, drinking too much, and showing favoritism to the cliques in the church. A circus atmosphere ruined what was designed to be the most memorable moments of worship a church family can enter into together. We must learn from their carnal display of disobedience. Each believer must examine his or her own heart before participating in the eating and drinking of the elements of the communion table.

## Water Baptism

Through the centuries, Christians have also declared their commitment to Christ by submitting themselves to water baptism, a public act of deep significance. Even though Romans 6 has reference to Spirit baptism, the word picture is appropriate for water baptism.

Or do you not know that all of us who have been baptized into Christ Jesus have been baptized into His death? (Rom. 6:3).

In the first century the term *baptism* meant "identification." In fact, it was a fuller's term—the dry cleaner of ancient days. When he took a white garment and dipped it into a scarlet dye, he was said to have "baptized" the garment. The white garment's identity was changed to scarlet. *Baptizo* was the term used when he changed its identity. That's the word used here, transliterated "baptized."

Or do you not know all of us who have been baptized into Christ Jesus have been baptized into His death? Therefore we have been buried with Him through baptism into death, in order that as Christ was raised from the dead through the glory of the Father, so we too might walk in newness of life (vv. 3-4).

Did you know that in the ordinance of baptism, the water is a picture of death? Have you ever been told that baptism is a picture of a person's identification with the death of Christ? It is true. It is symbolic of the resurrection of Christ out of death. The person being baptized is "acting out" his or her death to sin and subsequent newness of walk in Jesus Christ. This act of obedience isn't simply a take-it-or-leave-it issue. No. While it isn't essential for salvation, it is certainly expected of the believer. As with the Lord's Supper, it is a picture of our being united with Christ Jesus in the likeness of His death and His resurrection.

In my travels outside the United States, I have discovered that baptism is the most significant point of change in the eyes of the public. Internationally, the world believes that the one being baptized is indeed a Christian when he or she steps into the baptismal waters—a public testimony of faith in Christ. That act is a public declaration, saying, "I belong to Jesus Christ. I identify with His death for me. And by being raised from the water, I identify with a new kind of life that I could never live on my own, but by His power I will be able to experience. I've been born again. And that's why I want to display what has happened to me already in my life."

I appreciate the words that Philip Henry, father of Matthew Henry, wrote for his children. It became their baptismal statement:

I take God to be my chief end and highest good.
I take God the Son to my prince and Savior.
I take God the Holy Spirit to be my sanctifier,
teacher, guide, and comforter.
I take the Word of God to be my rule in all my actions
and the people of God to be my people
under all conditions.
I do hereby dedicate and devote to the Lord all I am,
all I have,
and all I can do.
And this I do deliberately, freely, and forever.

## Extending Your Roots

The ordinance of the Lord's Supper is a symbolic act of obedience. The death and second coming ofthe Lord are to be remembered.

1. To better understand what happened at that Passover meal in the upper room, read the following Gospel accounts.

Matthew 26:20-29
Mark 14:17-25
Luke 22:14-30
John 13:21-30

2. In his First Letter to the Corinthian church, Paul expressed his concern about participation in the Lord's Supper. Read 1 Corinthians 11:17-34. List some of Paul's specific instructions on how to observe the supper.

3. Jesus said, "This do in remembrance of Me." How do you personally remember Christ when you take the Lord's Supper in your church?

## Taproot

The ordinance of baptism is an enactment of faith—a personal faith in the death, burial, and resurrection of Jesus Christ.

1. Many Bible passages offer insight into this church ordinance. Read the following Scriptures and write a brief paragraph about each passage.
Matthew 3; 28:18-19

Acts 2:38; 8:14-16; 19:2-5

Galatians 3:25-27; Ephesians 4:4-6; Colossians 2:12.

2. Complete your study of baptism using resource books or a concordance.

# 13 Long Live God's People!

When we began this section I asked you to take charge of your thoughts. I'd like you to do that again as I close. I urge you to ask yourself several hard questions: Where do I really stand regarding the work of a local church? Is my participation halfhearted or wholehearted? Does my walk reflect its purity? Does my giving reflect generosity? Dig deeper. Probe your own heart. Have I taken the ordinances seriously as He has planned them to be taken? Have I prayed for the church's mission and ministry? Do I support it in active service, not simply in passive presence? Perhaps you have been overly critical of other ministries and too exclusive regarding your own. Maybe you have stopped attending any local church. Now is the time to deal with those things. Please do.

As you align yourself with the church, you join a body of people who have played a vital role in the shaping of history. They have often been maligned and misunderstood. They have occasionally been fanatical and unbalanced, at times ignored and at other times admired and quoted. But they have usually been sincere. Whatever, the church is God's project. It will not fail. Long live the church!

The following piece, though not original with me, sums up my convictions exactly:

> God has always had a people, a people who believe by faith, who trust and obey His Word, a people whose God is the Lord.

*Growing Deep in the Christian Life: The Family of God*

Many a foolish conqueror has made the mistake of thinking that because he had forced the Church of Jesus Christ out of sight, He had stilled its voice and snuffed out its life.

But God has always had a people; He has always had a people who believe; that believe His Word, a people whose God is the Lord.

The powerful current of a rushing river is not diminished because it is forced to flow underground. The purest water is the stream that bursts crystal clear into the sunlight after it has forced its way through solid rock.

There have been charlatans, like Simon the magician, who sought to barter on the open market that power which cannot be bought or sold. But, God has always had a people . . . men who could not be bought, and women who were beyond purchase. God has always had a people—people who believe by faith!

There have been times of affluence and prosperity when the Church's message has been diluted into oblivion by those who sought to make it socially attractive, neatly organized, and financially profitable.

It has been gold-plated, draped in purple, and encrusted with jewels. It has been misrepresented, ridiculed, lauded, and scorned.

These followers of Jesus Christ have been, according to the whim of the times, elevated as sacred leaders, and martyred as heretics. Yet, through it all there marches on that powerful army of the meek—God's chosen people who cannot be bought, flattered, murdered, or stilled! On through the ages they march!

God has always had a people—the Church, God's Church triumphant! God has always had a people, followers of Jesus—chosen people. A people who believe by faith, who trust and believe His Word, a people whose God is the Lord. God has always—*always*—had a people![1]

 *Extending Your Roots*

1. The Bible gives clear directives to the body of Christ. Prioritize the following directives. Read each verse and rate

the directives with 1 being something your church is absolutely doing—no doubt about it—and 12 indicating neglect. When this assignment is completed, you will have numbered these verses 1—12 in the order of importance.

_____ Ephesians 4:32
_____ Ephesians 4:16
_____ Colossians 3:9
_____ James 5:16
_____ 1 Corinthians 12:25
_____ 1 Thessalonians 5:11
_____ Ephesians 4:2
_____ Colossians 3:16
_____ Galatians 5:13
_____ 1 Peter 4:9
_____ Galatians 6:2
_____ Ephesians 5:21

2. Write some positive ways to improve what you ranked 10, 11, and 12.

*Taproot*

1. Write a prayer of gratitude to God for your church.

*Part*
**II**

*The
Family
of
God*

# 14 Encouragement Served Family Style

Did you ever get a song on your mind? Sure, it happens to all of us. I've had one on my mind for several days . . . ever since I returned from a weekend conference I spent with several hundred of our church folk at a Christian conference center in the mountains. It's not one of the great hymns of the church, but rather a very familiar folk song we sang during a fun time we spent together:

> O give me a home where the buffalo roam,
> Where the deer and the antelope play,
> Where seldom is heard a discouraging word,
> And the skies are not cloudy all day.

> Home, home on the range . . .

While turning that tune over in my mind all the way back from Forest Home, I began to think about that third line, "Where seldom is heard a discouraging word. " I asked myself: *Who wouldn't like to be in a home like that?* Unfortunately, we usually think of it as existing as a fantasy in some imaginary "Home on the Range." It's probably too ideal to be true. I thought, what we need is a place like that in the city . . . not on some idealistic blue-sky range far away. I also thought about the need for such a setting in the church today.

So I wrote another set of words that could be sung to the same tune.

> O give me a church where folks in the lurch
> Are encouraged, then healed from above;

**91**

Where seldom is heard a discouraging word,
And the truth is modeled in love.

Ever been in one like that? If you find one, I can guarantee the place will be packed to the rafters Sunday after Sunday. That kind of body will draw folks in like a magnet.
Why? Because we live in a world where the theme of life
seems to be putting people down, finding their faults, and
discouraging them.

 *Root Issues*

1. Hebrews 10:22 urges us to draw near to the Father!
Urges us to find cleansing and renewal through the blood of
Christ! Then, when we have been cleansed and sense the
nearness of our God, verses 24-25 urge us to pass that super-
natural encouragement along—family style! But it begins
with that vertical relationship between you and the Lord,
doesn't it? Have you "drawn near" to your Father today,
confidently claiming the blood of Jesus as your passport into
His presence? Hear His invitation in these verses and respond with all your heart.

2. Hebrews 10:24 suggests "let us consider" how to stimulate and encourage one another. In other words, it takes
some careful, creative thought—it doesn't happen automatically. I like the way *The Amplified Bible* renders it:

> And let us consider and give attentive, continuous care to
> watching over one another, studying how we may stir up
> (stimulate and incite) to love and helpful deeds and noble
> activities.

Think of three individuals you would like to encourage
over the next few weeks. Now, do what the text says —consider. Think and pray it through. Seek discernment from
the Holy Spirit to discover practical, appropriate methods.
And then perform a courage transfusion!

3. In this chapter and those that follow, we'll look at the
awesome power of the "encouraging word." Scriptures like

Matthew 12:36-37 and Ephesians 4:29 underline what Solomon wrote again and again in the Proverbs. If you have the courage, ask a close friend or associate or spouse to comment on the content of your casual conversation since they have known you. Are your words generally positive, "edifying," encouraging? What steps could you take to both "monitor" your speech and turn it in a direction that builds others and praises God?

4. Looking for something to read when you finish this book something that might help you cultivate your own private worship of the Lord? For an unforgettable experience, dip into the writings of A. W. Tozer. Classics such as *The Pursuit of God*, or *Worship: The Missing Jewel of the Evangelical Church* are available through your local Christian bookstore—or perhaps your church library.

5. Is the music of worship a part of your daily life? Choose a few choruses, Scripture songs, or perhaps a grand old hymn or two to commit to memory. Then, rediscover the joy of singing your praise and adoration back to the Lord. Why let "the professionals" on your stereo or car radio have all the privilege of making music for the King. Don't worry if you can't carry a tune. If your spirit is in harmony with His, the music will be beautiful . . . and God will be well pleased. Let it shine!

6. You may or may not be pleased with all the aspects of the "worship service" at your church. Nevertheless, you can worship—with all your heart! Make up your mind on Sunday morning that you *will* worship the Lord through every aspect of the service—through the singing, the offering, the praying, and the preaching. Refuse to let distractions or wandering thoughts pull your attention and concentration away from the living God and His Word. Give yourself totally to the worship of your God and Savior during those brief minutes. Let that hour of worship set the pace for the rest of your week.

*Growing Deep in the Christian Life: The Family of God*

Within the family of God, you will find many discouraged people. They need help and the best help a family member can give is encouragement.

Read 1 Thessalonians 5:11.

1. The following situations are about discouraged people in the family of God. Read each situation and decide on a first step you could take in offering encouragement.

- A wife is discouraged because her husband won't come to church with her.
- Deacon Perry lost his job two weeks ago.
- A Sunday School teacher's teenage son was arrested for possession of drugs Saturday night.
- A child has failing grades again.
- Jerry and Beth broke up and Beth doesn't have a date for the youth banquet.
- Virgina's mother needs full-time care and there is no extra money.
- Don's wife left him.
- Add discouraged people from your family of God.

1. First Thessalonians 5:11-28 includes some specific examples of how we can encourage other people. Read these verses and apply the examples to the situations you have just read.

2. Focus on verse 18. How would you explain this passage to a discouraged person?

# 15 | Encouragement Defined and Explained

I checked with Webster and found that the verb *discourage* means "to deprive of courage, to dishearten, to hinder, to deter." And, in contrast, the same source defines *encourage* as "to inspire with courage, to give spirit or hope; hearten, to spur on, stimulate, to give help."

When I analyze the English word *encouragement*, my thoughts turn to the word *enthusiasm*. The Greek term *entheos* is the root. It means "to put God (theos) into (en) something or someone." Since that is true, then *encourage* would mean "to put courage into someone." You may be surprised to discover who needs it. Sometimes the most unexpected people you could imagine need it.

While I was hurrying to get away for the conference at Forest Home, I whipped through the mail at home and found my copy of *Sports Illustrated*. I shoved it into my briefcase since I knew there would be some time to relax on Saturday afternoon up in the mountains. Sure enough, I was able to curl up in a corner with a cup of coffee and browse through the new issue—one of my favorite pastimes. While reading it, I came across a gripping story of a relatively unknown athlete—a young man named Brian Hiemer.

Nebraska football players will wear the numeral 94 on their helmets this season in tribute to senior Brian Hiemer, 21, who died after shooting himself in the head on August 13, the day he was to report for fall practice. Hiemer's death shocked an entire state. "Nobody wanted to believe what happened," says Bill Morgan, owner of the A and B Cafe in

95

Shelby, Nebraska . . . Hiemer's hometown. "Everyone wants to know why."

The article continues:

> An all-state kicker and tight end as well as a yearbook editor and prom king, Hiemer had a storybook high school career. At Nebraska he was dubbed the Comeback Kid. When he was cut after his freshman season, he persuaded head coach Tom Osborne to give him another chance, he then rose rapidly from 10th on the Cornhusker depth charts to first string. . . .

After describing his great season last year, it ends:

> Hiemer had returned to the family's 320-acre farm from the university on Friday evening, August 9. Over the weekend, he mowed the lawn and walked the fields with his father. On Tuesday, however, Loyola Hiemer noticed that her son was unusually restless and quiet. That afternoon, while his father was in the north fields and his mother was in the house, Hiemer walked behind a wooden shed and sat down with a .22 caliber rifle, one bullet in the weapon. He was found about 4 p.m. by his father. Walking near the shed last week, Willard Hiemer said, "You look for something, a warning. Maybe there was a reason, but Brian didn't tell us."
>
> . . . Kriss King, a classmate who dated him last spring, says that Hiemer, with an eye on a pro career, was trying unsuccessfully to put on extra weight. . . . King and Gregg Reeves, a defensive end, both say that Hiemer was worried about a future life on the farm. "He didn't think that with just him and his dad it was economically feasible," says Reeves. . . .
>
> Nebraska is now preparing for the season opener against Florida State this Saturday, September 7, but the team has already suffered its biggest loss of the season. Hiemer is gone, and no one understands the reason. Huey says, "Whatever it was, it will rest with Brian."[1]

Frankly, that could be your son, or mine.

It could be your roommate, or maybe your neighbor. Could be your own mom or dad. Could be the person who sits right next to you in church on Sunday. Who would have ever imagined?

I don't mean to be dramatic about it, but this business of discouragement is real. It hits like a silent plague and cripples us within. I cannot emphasize enough the importance of those words:

> Give me a church where folks in the lurch
> Are encouraged, then healed from above;
> Where seldom is heard a discouraging word,
> And the truth is modeled in love.

That isn't some dreamy idea that comes out of a theoretical mind. That comes straight out of the Scriptures. Did you know that we are actually *commanded* by our God to encourage one another? He expects us to serve it to one another "family style."

Believe me, if we in God's family fail to do it, it is doubtful we'll find it anywhere else.

 *Extending Your Roots*

An encouraging person should be able to express sincere enthusiasm.

1. Write a definition of these words:

Encouragement:


Enthusiasm:


2. Based on your definitions, check the characteristics of an encourager that apply to you.

_____ I can see how a discouraged person can become encouraged.

_____ I enjoy encouraging people.

*Growing Deep in the Christian Life: The Family of God*

_____ I look for the good in each person in contrast to what is bad.

_____ I can keep myself from being discouraged.

_____ I can see the positive potential of people and comment on it to them.

3. In your opinion, are you an enthusiastic, encouraging person?

4. What have you done recently to encourage someone?

## *Taproot*

1. First Samuel 1 records an interesting experience in the family of God. There is an interchanging of encouragement/discouragement. Read the story and explain the many ways *Elkanah, Hannah,* and *Peninnah* were:

DISCOURAGED                                    ENCOURAGED

# 16 Biblical Basis for Encouragement

The Scripture I want us to look at first is Hebrews 10. All the way through this letter the spotlight has been upon Jesus Christ, the Superior One. He has opened for us a new and living way to the Father. We don't have to go through a system of works. We don't have to go through some other person who will represent our cause. We don't have to earn our way into the presence of God and hope that He will lend an ear and hear our requests. No, not that. Finally, the climax:

> Since therefore, brethren, we have confidence to enter the holy place by the blood of Jesus, by a new and living way which He inaugurated for us through the veil, that is, His flesh, and since we have a great priest over the house of God (vv. 19-21).

His point is this: Since we have confidence to enter the Lord's presence and since we have Christ as our "great priest," let us execute the following three commands, each of which is introduced by "Let us . . ."

> Let us draw near with a sincere heart in full assurance of faith, having our hearts sprinkled clean from an evil conscience and our bodies washed with pure water (v. 22).

This is symbolic language. It means: Let us come into the presence of our God clean and pure. Let's have no lingering sin hanging heavily over us like an anchor as we attempt to storm the throne with our needs. Let us draw near!

The next command:

99

> Let us hold fast the confession of our hope without waver-
> ing, for He who promised is faithful (v. 23).

This second command is a strong one, written before the ink
is dry on the first. "Let us draw near." Amen! "Let us hold
fast." Amen! But also:

> And let us consider how to stimulate one another to love
> and good deeds (v. 24).

Did you ever know that was in the Bible? Let us give attention on *how* we might stimulate our brothers and sisters in
the family of God. It isn't just a suggestion, an off-the-cuff,
casual idea like, "Oh, by the way, it might be good, while
you're holding fast to the faith, to toss in a little
encouragement."

But he's not through with the thought. It is completed in
the next verse:

> Not forsaking our own assembling together, as is the habit
> of some, but encouraging one another; and all the more, as
> you see the day drawing near (v. 25).

It is impossible to stimulate someone else to love and good
deeds if we are not around them. We cannot be an encouragement if we live our lives in secret caves, pushing people
away from us. People out of touch don't encourage others.
Encouragement is a face-to-face thing. So, in effect, he says:

> Let us not neglect our church meetings, as some people do,
> but encourage and warn each other, especially now that the
> day of his coming back again is drawing near (v. 25, TLB)

I see a couple of thoughts woven through these lines.

*1. Encouragement is not the responsibility of a gifted few,
but the responsibility of all in the family of God.* Obviously,
the official role of a pastor is the responsibility of a few. And
the role of an elder or deacon is another responsibility for a
few. Maybe an officer or a teacher is the responsibility of a
few people in a church. But I don't find this passage addressed to any specific, gifted individual, rather to all in the
family. That means you.

*2. Encouragement is not something that is needed less in*

*the body, but more.* You'll notice that the writer refers to this being needed "all the more as you see the day [of Christ's return] drawing near." Do you know why? It is mentioned in 2 Timothy 3:1.

> This know also, that in the last days perilous times shall come (KJV).

Interesting word that Paul uses, translated "perilous" in the *King James Version.* "Troublesome" is the paraphrase that some will use. It is also like our English term *savage.* "In the last days, savage times will come." These are the days in which we live.

Now why do I emphasize that? Because that's the reason we need encouragement all the more. Like early American pioneers who braved the new frontiers, when we walk out of the loving fellowship of God's family, we move into "savage territory." In that realm we are threatened and we can be easily intimidated. In light of that fact, God's people need to turn on the encouragement! The family of God is not a place for verbal put-downs, sarcastic jabs, critical comments, and harsh judgment. We get enough of that from the world. This is a place we need to assemble for the purpose of being encouraged . . . a place we are free to be ourselves.

One New Testament scholar does a fine job of tracing the meaning of encouragement through the New Testament. He points out how it was used in extra-biblical literature for exhorting troops who were about to go into battle.

> Euripides . . . describing the plans for battle says: "So they did hail them, *cheering* them to fight." Xenophon, uses it of urging the soldiers to embark upon the ships and set out on an adventurous voyage . . . Polybius uses it of . . . Demetrius rallying his men and addressing the ranks before they embarked upon battle . . . And the word he uses of embarking upon battle is *Diakinduneuein,* which means to accept the risk of battle.
>
> Again and again we find that *Parakalein* is the word of the rallying-call; it is the word used of the speeches of leaders and of soldiers who urge each other on. It is the word used of

words which send fearful and timorous and hesitant soldiers and sailors courageously into battle. A *Parakletos* is therefore an *Encourager,* one who puts courage into the fainthearted, one who nerves the feeble arm for fight, one who makes a very ordinary man cope gallantly with a perilous and a dangerous situation. . . .

. . . The word *Parakalein* is the word for exhorting [others] to noble deeds and high thoughts; it is especially the word of courage before battle. Life is always calling us into battle and the one who makes us able to stand up to the opposing forces, to cope with life and to conquer life is the *Parakletos*, the Holy Spirit, who is none other than the presence and power of the risen Christ.[1]

*Parakalein*—that's the word that is most often translated "encourage" in our Bibles. We find it again in Hebrews 10:25.

Not forsaking our own assembling together, as is the habit of some, but encouraging one another.

Celeste Holm, a film star of yesteryear, was quoted on one occasion as saying, "We live by encouragement, and we die without it—slowly, sadly, angrily."

Why would I address this issue in a book on doctrine? Because I have observed how easy it is for Christians to become attracted to theological truths to the exclusion of close relationships with each other. We need both/and, not either/or. The place of strong spiritual instruction is also to be a place of deep, personal compassion. The same Scriptures that encourage our growing in knowledge also exhort us to grow in love, tolerance, grace, and acceptance. Those passages that urge keen thinking and clear discernment are well balanced by other passages that affirm our understanding and, yes, our encouraging one another.

Blind songwriter Ken Medema seldom fails to put his finger on a tender nerve. His lack of eyesight has sensitized his insight, giving him that sixth sense we who see often miss. I love his song "If This Is Not a Place," which says everything that I am trying to communicate, only so much better.

If this is not a place where tears are understood,
Then where shall I go to cry?
And if this is not a place where my spirit can take wings,
Then where shall I go to fly?
I don't need another place for tryin' to impress you
With just how good and virtuous I am, no, no, no
I don't need another place for always bein' on top of things
Everybody knows that it's a sham, it's a sham.
I don't need another place for always wearin' smiles
Even when it's not the way I feel.
I don't need another place to mouth the same old platitudes
Everybody knows that it's not real.
So if this is not a place where my questions can be asked,
Then where shall I go to seek?
And if this is not a place where my heart cry can be heard,
Where, tell me where, shall I go to speak?
So if this is not a place where tears are understood,
Where shall I go, where shall I go to fly?[2]

 *Extending Your Roots*

The Book of Ruth gives us a picture of a nontraditional family. The experiences shared by Ruth and Naomi offer a look at how to deal with encouragement and discouragement within a family.

1. Read the book and write down the evidences of encouragement from Ruth to Naomi and Naomi to Ruth.

RUTH                                              NAOMI

2. Five steps to being an encourager are developed in Ruth's experiences:

● She really cared for Naomi. Is there someone you really care for who is discouraged? Who?

● She did something about the situation. What would you need to do to become an encourager for the person you know who is discouraged?

● She didn't criticize Naomi for being "down." How can you show respect for a person's feelings?

● She led Naomi to believe, "You can do it." How can you lead your acquaintance to believe in himself?

● She helped Naomi experience God's great blessing on them both—a son and grandson. How can you declare to your discouraged friend God's love and goodness?

 *Taproot*

1. The apostle Paul wrote to the church in Rome about personal responsibility especially to the family of God. Read Romans 12. Notice what Paul wrote about spiritual gifts.

2. Verse 8 mentions the gift of encouraging others. Using a concordance, find out more about this particular gift. Is this gift referred to by another name?

3. Do you know what your spiritual gifts are?

4. Perhaps you would like to learn more about spiritual gifts. Purchase books from a Christian book store or visit your church library and pursue the subject.

# 17 Encouragement: How to Do It

For the next few pages, I want us to limit our thoughts on encouragement to the *tongue*. I want us to see, as if for the very first time, how much weight is carried by the words we utter and the tone we use. To keep it simple, let's stay in the Book of Proverbs, the wisdom book. Think of these words as God's counsel to all of us in His family, for indeed they are.

### Proverbs 10:11-13

The mouth of the righteous is a fountain of life, but the mouth of the wicked conceals violence. Hatred stirs up strife, but love covers all transgressions (vv. 11-12).

We cannot deny that the tongue is an instrument of forgiveness. It has the ability to conceal violence and cover transgressions. Continuing on:

On the lips of the discerning, wisdom is found (v. 13*a*).

There is a transfer of wisdom from one life to another through the vehicle of the tongue.

What power! A fountain of life. An instrument of forgiveness. A concealment of violence. A source and/or transfer of wisdom.

### Proverbs 10:19-21

When there are many words, transgression is unavoidable, But he who restrains his lips is wise (v. 19).

I'm glad God included those words in His Book. It is easy to think that all we need to do when we're together is talk,

talk, talk. Sometimes well-chosen words, though brief, are much more eloquent than a paragraph of information dumped from someone's mouth to another's ears. Proverbs 10:19 extols rationing our words.

He continues:

> The tongue of the righteous is as choice silver. . . . The lips of the righteous feed many (vv. 20-21).

The tongue, with words as valuable as choice silver, brings treasured nourishment to hungry hearts.

### Proverbs 12:17-18

> He who speaks truth tells what is right, But a false witness, deceit. There is one who speaks rashly like the thrusts of a sword, But the tongue of the wise brings healing.

I don't know if you have been the recipient of healing from someone's tongue, but I certainly have. Perhaps you can recall being hurt so deeply the wound refused to heal. No scab would form within. And about the time it started to heal, it got ripped off again. You bleed. You're uncomfortable. You may be humiliated, perhaps frightened by the savage world around you. And someone in God's forever family cares enough to look deep into your eyes and say just the right thing at just the right time. What happens? "The tongue of the wise brings healing."

I can't emphasize enough the importance of the ways moms and dads talk with their children. As a matter of fact, I was really caught off guard when I first found this next proverb. You talk about a reproof from God, I got it! And I have never forgotten it.

### Proverbs 18:21

> Death and life are in the power of the tongue, And those who love it will eat its fruit.

In recent years I have come to know and have grown to love and respect Gordon MacDonald. I now consider Gordon one of my friends. The man has written one of the finest books on parenting ever published. It is entitled *The Effective Father*. I have read and reread sections of this book so much, they are now ripped and ragged. I always stop at this illustration, since it describes a scene so typical, so painful in lives today.

> A forty-two-year-old man has allowed me to look into the inner recesses of his life and see what makes him what he is today: a man who is frantically working himself into exhaustion; one who spends every dime he makes for impressive artifacts of luxury and success; a volatile human being whose temper explodes at the slightest hint of disagreement or criticism. As we talk I ask Tom to tell me about his childhood.
>
> At one impressionable point in boyhood, when my friend was apparently displeasing his father with the way he was doing a chore, his father said to him, "Tom, you will always be a bum. You're not going to amount to a thing; you're a bum!" Tom goes on to tell me that whenever he and his father had angry moments, the same prediction would be repeated until it burned its way into the boy's spirit so deeply that, like shrapnel embedded in flesh, the words could never be removed. Thirty years later, Tom still suffers from his father's verbal malpractice. They drive him day and night from a subconscious source to attempt to prove that his father was wrong. Ironically, even though Tom's father is dead, the habit patterns of Tom's inner life still maintain fever pitch to convince a dead father and a slightly unsure Tom that he is not a bum. Let anyone suggest to Tom that he is doing something wrong or that he is deficient in some aspect of his life, and hostility, defensiveness, and furious energy are unleashed to guard against what he senses is a resurrection of the old accusations from a thoughtless father who verbally set a wrong pace.[2]

Moms and dads, pastors and teachers, counselors and coaches, your tongue possesses the power of life and death. Let us never think our words will be overlooked and easily erased. You and I can remember a statement from a teacher who, in a moment of haste, said something that pierced our hearts and ripped its way in, leaving a scar. It will never be fully forgotten.

We can't change yesterday, but, my, the possibilities that await us tomorrow! Maybe your son or your daughter is now grown or almost grown. Don't wait another day . . . start now! *It is never too late to start doing what is right.*

I have discovered that an encouraging church family is such because its homes are that. Let me ask you: Is *yours* an encouraging home? If I were to drop by as an invisible guest and listen in on conversations, would I hear sarcasm, put-downs, and caustic comments? Or would I hear, "Good job! I notice you're growing up. What a delight you are to our family. How pleased I am to see that you have begun to master such-and-such skill"? Or, "I know you've failed, and I understand. I've been there. It'll be better tomorrow. Let me work with you. Let me help you."

"Death and life are in the power of the tongue." Think of it this way: *Death words* destroy, hurt, create hateful and humiliating feelings. *Life words* build and increase strength of character. They lift spirits. They center on the truth; therefore, they set the person free who would otherwise be in bondage.

Would you like a brief definition of encouragement? In two words, it is a *courage transfusion.* Every time we encourage someone, we give them a transfusion of courage.

That could create a problem. In order for courage to be transferred, the one doing the transferring has to have sufficient inner strength and must be secure enough, confident enough, resourceful enough to provide a surplus to someone else. That explains why unforgiving, fighting, critical people are not encouragers. Only those who are excited about life can transfer courage. People who are down on themselves, uncertain regarding their own self-image, can't do that.

*Growing Deep in the Christian Life: The Family of God*

# Extending Your Roots

My tongue plays a major role in how I encourage or discourage a person.

1. Read aloud this paraphrase, "Don't talk so much! You keep putting your foot in your mouth. Be sensible and turn off the flow" (Prov. 10:19, TLB).

There are many verbal exchanges in the Scripture that teach us how to be encouragers . . . how to say the right thing at the right time. Also some not-so-encouraging situations are presented.

2. Study the following passages. Write the encouraging or discouraging words that are said and the reaction of the person.

John 20:24-28

Matthew 27:3-5

Matthew 15:21-28

John 21:15-17

*Encouragement: How to Do It*

 — *Taproot*

1. Read James 3:1-12 and complete the following assignment.
- The tongue is like _____ .
- Ways to control the tongue are _____ .
- My tongue gives me the most trouble _____ .
- I used my tongue to encourage _____ .
- I used my tongue to discourage _____ .

2. Lord, help me to control my tongue.
Lead me to _____ .

# 18 A Classic Example of an Encourager

If you are like me, you appreciate seeing biblical principles illustrated in the lives of biblical characters. I've chosen one of our favorites—David.

While still a teenager he killed the giant Goliath, a story familiar to most people. But what followed is not as well known. That heroic act shocked the king whose name was Saul. He didn't even know who young David was when the event occurred. But once that deed was done, *everybody* in Israel became familiar with the young giant killer. Eventually, he joined the king's staff.

Within a few hours the people of Israel composed a simple song: "Saul has slain his thousands, And David his ten thousands!" (1 Sam. 18:7).

Everybody (but one) sang that tune. Everybody (but one) applauded the accomplishment. Saul hated that song, because *he* wanted the people's applause. He was too insecure to see someone else promoted above him in popularity. What happened? Exactly what you would expect. Saul began to watch him. His intense jealousy increased his suspicion. And before long the paranoia turned to hate, then to rage, and finally to thoughts of murder. Saul took a spear and literally tried to kill him. David was forced to run for his life. For over a dozen years (!) David lived as a fugitive, hiding from Saul.

Ironically, in the meantime, Saul's son Jonathan developed a close relationship with David. It was a deep relationship of love—genuine love. "He loved him," says verse 3, "as he loved himself." Unlike his father, Jonathan had a strong self-image, hence he was able to give himself to David. They became "soul mates." They understood each other. Their lives fit together like teeth in gears. They didn't have to explain themselves. They were completely at home in each other's presence. They loved each other deeply.

But all the while Saul's intensity increased. Finally, David is driven into the wilderness like a wild animal, not knowing where to turn. His fear is reaching maximum proportions. Disillusioned, confused, and hunted, David is near the breaking point. At that moment, Jonathan arrived on the scene with a "courage transfusion."

> Now David became aware that Saul had come out to seek his life while David was in the wilderness of Ziph at Horesh (1 Sam. 23:15).

Before reading any further, take a moment to identify with David in the wilderness. Every sunset added to his panic. Each new dawn introduced another day of running, watching, escaping, hiding. With relentless determination, Saul and his army pursued him. Next verse:

> And Jonathan, Saul's son, arose and went to David at Horesh, and encouraged him in God (v. 16).

The Hebrew term for *encouraged* conveys the idea of putting strength into someone's hand, arms, or body, so they can resist a pressure or an attack. Not waiting for an invitation, Jonathan arose and sought out David. To do what? To pass along fresh courage and new strength. Why? Because he loved him.

There are times you'll have to swim upstream to bring encouragement. Usually, it is unnecessary to wait for an invitation. Let me pass along a simple little formula about encouragement. It isn't original with me. "Words that encourage are inspired by love and directed toward fear." The source of that statement is a fine book entitled *Encouragement: The Key to Caring*.

> It is a mistake to think of encouragement as a set of specific words or phrases. Encouragement depends less on which

words we use than the motivation behind them. Words that encourage are inspired by love and directed toward fear. These two conditions must be met for words to encourage.[1]

Let's look at the two conditions. Condition one: Words that encourage are inspired by love, not by fear; that is, the words spoken must never function as a "layer" for the speaker. Condition two: Words that encourage are aimed not at another's "layers" with the intent of rearranging them, but rather at another's hidden fear with the intent of reducing it. Read those thoughts again, slowly. It's extremely important that you grasp both conditions. I'll explain it further in a moment.

That is what makes Jonathan's time with David so significant. He really loved him. His presence and words conveyed the feelings, "I love you, David. I believe in you." And when he came to David, David didn't hide the truth and say, "Hey, I'm not afraid. I'll take on Saul and his army. Why in the world are you here?" He didn't fake it and try to act strong. David was scared. And in the presence of his friend, he didn't hide it. Nor did Jonathan hide his motivation. "David, I love you too much to leave you alone." David's response must have been, "Jonathan, how I need you right now! Thank you for coming."

Let me show you in a few words what I'm trying to say by referring to the four levels of encouragement in the chart on the next page. For a few moments think in terms of "layers" and "core." Unfortunately, most of us build layers around ourselves. Most of us give off an air of being on top of things. We're winning. We've got life by the tail. We can handle it. And so we give superficial comments to people, and we respond superficially in return, from layer to layer, and that doesn't bring encouragement.

I can just hear the fellow who's had a coaching background. He's a tough guy, and he's got a son who weight 101 pounds, who is hoping to be a running back for a high school football team that's full of 200-pound-plus football players. And the little kid is scared out of his mind . . . but he can't

*A Classic Example of an Encourager*

**ENCOURAGEMENT SERVED FAMILY STYLE**

LEVELS OF ENCOURAGEMENT

| | |
|---|---|
| FEAR → FEAR | NO ENCOURAGEMENT |
| FEAR → FEAR | SUPERFICIAL ENCOURAGEMENT |
| LOVE → FEAR | LIMITED ENCOURAGEMENT |
| LOVE → FEAR | EFFECTIVE ENCOURAGEMENT |

*(See Crabb and Allender, Encouragement, 72-73)*

tell his daddy he's scared. Every morning his daddy says to him, "Suck it up, Bucko." And junior says, "Right, Dad." As he walks out of the house for school to catch the bus, the kid is scared to death. He's thinking about facing the team that afternoon in practice. But he can't admit his fear to his dad because his dad doesn't leave room for that. We're talking layer-to-layer relationship, which brings *no* encouragement. Look at the chart. This relationship is illustrated at the top level.

There's another level. It's a level of fear inside one individual, but somehow that same person can penetrate beneath the layer of another person and reach the true fear within. That's what we might call "superficial encouragement." Behind a shield of success and false security, we can come across with right words, even quoting verses and telling someone we'll pray for them in their fear or in their need. But that, at best, brings only *superficial* encouragement. It does not last. By the way, a meaningful relationship is not developed between those two people even though right words—even scriptural words—were spoken.

There's a third level, where the person doing the encouraging really does love the other individual, but somehow can't bring himself to say it. So in another guise he or she will communicate to the fear of this individual, and that brings *limited* encouragement. And it lasts a little longer, but it's never permanent.

The best kind of encouragement (represented at the bottom of the chart) is when the person doing the encouraging genuinely loves the other individual and expresses it. That's our friend Jonathan. In such situations the person needing encouragement honestly admits his fear, which causes a meaningful connection between the two. In that situation, soul meets with soul. And the deepest level of needs begins to be met. *That* is our goal—*effective* encouragement served family style!

When "layered" Christians meet together and everyone remains hidden beneath invisible masks and protected behind untouchable walls, nothing is really accomplished by way of encouragement. Everyone maneuvers his or her way through the maze of unspoken feelings, unwilling to admit the truth. What an unsatisfying, strained encounter! It's about as satisfying as kissing someone with a pane of glass between you, or taking a shower with a raincoat on. But it goes on in churches year after year.

Is it ever possible for me to encourage myself?

Yes, as a matter of fact, I think that the more we operate on this fourth level, the more we are able to give ourselves a transfusion of courage when necessary. I do not believe, however, that we ever reach the place where we never need some kind of encouragement from someone else. If we did, we wouldn't have the command in Hebrews 10:25 to "encouraging one another, and all the more as you see the day drawing near." But there are times we must encourage ourselves. When you travel a little further into David's biography, you see that he came to a place where everything, it seemed, had broken loose in his life. Not only was he exhausted from battle, the enemy had ransacked his home and kidnnaped his wife and children. Even his men entertained thoughts of mutiny. Jonathan wasn't around to give his friend a "courage transfusion." David was all alone. We read that "David strengthened himself in the Lord his God" (1 Sam. 30:6).

I have discovered that when I haven't anyone near me upon whom I can call, when I'm all alone, I find the Book of Psalms my most consistent source of encouragement. When I turn to the psalms, it is amazing how much courage is poured into my soul. Often, it is as if God were speaking directly to my immediate needs. Have you made the same discovery?

Another source of personal encouragement is the hymnbook. I happen to love the hymns, especially the grand old hymns, many of which I've committed to memory. I will often pray through a song or a hymn. And somehow in the rhythm, the meter, the profoundly personal message of that music, I find my heart lifted up . . . another "courage transfusion" occurs.

 *Extending Your Roots*

1. Joseph, son of Jacob, is a classic example of an encourager. His life recorded in Genesis 37—50, is interwoven with people and places. His ability to encourage others is unique. Read this passage in your Bible and place a small check mark in the margin by each evidence of encouragement. Also put a minus sign by times of discouragement.

2. Why is Hebrews 11:22 a verse about encouragement?

*Growing Deep in the Christian Life: The Family of God*

3. Do you believe that encouragers are people of genuine faith in God? Explain.

 *Taproot*

1. Another experience of David is a classic example of a self-encourager. Read about his need for courage in 1 Samuel 24 and how he encouraged himself in the related Psalm 57.

2. Could you create a psalm of encouragement for your life today or in the future? Try.

# **19** Three Crucial Questions Regarding Encouragement

Let's wrap up our thoughts on encouragement with three crucial questions.

*1. Who should I attempt to encourage?* Ideally, everyone I meet; but realistically, those with whom I have established a close relationship. By the way, don't think that is automatic. You know with whom I am closest? My wife and my four children. You know who are often *last* to get encouragement from me (I confess with some embarrassment)? My wife and my four children. Yet I cannot overstate the value of "courage transfusion" among family members.

I challenge you to recall the last time you deliberately gave encouragement to your mate. There wasn't any hint dropped. No pleading invitation. Because of an understanding of his or her fear, you stepped in and extended a statement of strength. And how about your children? Or a very close friend? Let's not assume others don't need it, even though they don't drop hints.

*2. How can the levels be penetrated?* I'll answer that with three "progressive" answers.

- It always takes time.
- It usually involves pain.
- It occasionally can be addressed verbally (i.e., "I sense you're hiding. As I talk with you right now, I sense that you're not really helping me see what's going on. Something is being held back").

That explains why it has to be a close relationship. You don't walk up to a stranger and say those words. You say them only to those with whom a deep level of love and acceptance has been cultivated.

*3. What essential techniques need to be remembered?*

- Talk less so you can feel more.
- Be sensitive to the timing.
- Watch your wording.
- Do everything in your power not to judge (we can say we're encouraging, but we're really preaching).
- Examine your motive.
- Guard against sarcasm.
- Don't hide behind a layer.

Remember the primary principle: **Words that encourage are inspired by love and directed toward fear.**

I close with a story that could be my own, but I prefer to use another's. You should have little difficulty identifying with it.

My wife and I had drooled over a planned sailing vacation for more than a year. Sacrificing a few pleasures and hoarding our pennies helped us to afford a week on the west coast of Florida at a sailing school. A week of sheer joy—rich time together, fun on the water, and rejoicing in God's blessings—rewarded our long anticipation.

When the week was over, we returned to the wintry climate of our northern home. Moving quickly from tropical paradise to snow-covered streets proved to be a major culture shock. I was mature enough to accept the loss of paradise without slipping into a sulk or depression, but I did feel a grudging reluctance as I dragged myself back to work bundled up in overcoat and gloves. An appeal to "rejoice evermore" or to "fight the good fight" would not have moved me at that moment. I was mildly down.

Eavesdrop on two conversations that took place shortly after my return home:

Fred: "Looks like you got some sun."

Dan: "Becky and I just spent a week in Florida. Great weather. We went sailing for a week."

Fred: "Jet set life, huh? Must be doing better than most of us. Too bad the tan won't last up here." (Fred then laughed a decidedly sarcastic laugh.)

Dan: "I know, but it was worth it just to get away, relax, and spend time together. It's hard though to get back to the grind of . . ."

Fred: " 'Grind!' At least you got away! Well, look, we better figure out when we can get together to work on that project that's due . . ."

Before the conversation I was mildly discouraged. Afterward I was moderately discouraged—less inclined to return to my responsibilities, more affected by the realities of a sometimes unpleasant life. Why? Fred is a friend of mind. He is not typically unkind toward me. Nor did he seem especially vindictive or angry during our interchange. Yet his words were discouraging.

Fred was wrapped up in his world, unconcerned about the effect of his words on me, insensitive to what I was feeling. He never acknowledged my emotions, he battered them. Rather than express understanding, he scorned my sluggishness. He failed to give me a perspective to help me carry on; instead he reminded me of my duties.

Listen to the other conversation:

Jane: "Hi, Dan! Hey, good tan! When did you get back?"

Dan: "Just two days ago."

Jane: "How was it—a good time?"

Dan: "I was great! Just what Becky and I needed to unwind. Makes it hard to come back though. After eighty-degree days, below zero is hard to take."

Jane: "I'll bet! Probably hard to believe you were even there. How's Becky taking her reentry to the real world?"

Dan: "Better than me [sic], I think. Her schedule up here is tough, but a little more flexible than mine. I feel the contrast between having nothing to do for a week and having to meet time demands again."

Jane: "So you're the struggling one now."

Dan: "I'm not proud of it, but I am."

Jane: "Your school and work schedule is really pretty demanding of your time, isn't it?"

Dan: "Becky and I had so much undisturbed time just to be together—and up here I'm lucky if I get any quality time with her at all. I'm afraid our commitments to other things might damage some of the closeness we feel with each other."

Jane: "So it's not just missing warm weather and sailing that's getting you."

Dan: "I guess not. Maybe the trip helped me realize that my priorities were out of line, and now I'm afraid I'll get them fouled up again."

He concludes:

> The contrast between the first and second conversations is dramatic, but not overdone. They happened just that way. Jane made an effort to understand me. She esteemed another's concerns greater than her own. She responded to my needs rather than to hers. Her encouraging words prompted me to evaluate what my struggles really were. With a better grip on my real problem clarifying the challenge that lay before me, I felt a renewed sense of commitment to keep my life in order. Jane had stirred me to love and good deeds.[2]

Yes, no doubt about it, doctrinal knowledge is important. We need to know what we believe and why we believe it. A church stands firmer amidst stormy times when its members are doctrinally sound. But no amount of doctrine will replace our need for encouraging relationships built on love and understanding.

Knowledge may strengthen, but relationships soften. A healthy church family has both.

# Extending Your Roots

1. When we encourage others we serve Christ. Examples for us "wanna-be-encouragers" are found in Mark 5. Jesus encouraged several groups or individuals. Read the chapter and express in your words how He encouraged others.

*GROUP/INDIVIDUAL     EXAMPLE*

verse 1

verse 22

verse 25

verse 40

2. Are there any lessons from that this chapter that you can learn? Be specific.

 *Taproot*

Read each characteristic and relate that description to a verse or person in the Bible.

An encourager
- is willing to take risks.
- has the ability to see Christ in others.
- is patient and hard working.
- knows how to perform simple acts to help others.
- is a person of faith.

2. Remember Barnabas, the encourager. Read Acts 11:24. Do you see yourself in this verse?

# 20

# Worship:
# Let It Shine!
# Let It Shine!

It happened in Canada way back in 1961. A group of ministers had gathered for a special series of meetings. They had invited one of their favorite preachers. He was not a physically impressive individual or one known for his charisma and eloquence. But he was one who knew God and walked closely with Him.

From 1928 to 1959 the man had pastored what some might call a rather inconspicuous church in Chicago, the Southside Alliance Church. During those thirty-one years he had emerged, in the opinion of many, as the conscience of evangelicalism at large. The preacher was Aiden Wilson Tozer. He preferred, simply, A. W. Tozer.

There was a little surprise as that wiry soldier of the cross stood in front of those Canadian churchmen and announced his subject. And had I been one of the ministers, perhaps I, too, would have been surprised at the topic he chose—WORSHIP. I mean, after all, that is a minister's craft. That's like talking to a group of auto mechanics about car engines, like talking to musicians about the chromatic scale. But how much there was to learn! How long lasting those messages have become! So significant were they that they have been put into a booklet that is still available today, as are most of Tozer's works.

One line from his message on worship is as meaningful today as it was the day he said it, perhaps more: "Worship is the missing jewel of the evangelical church."

Even though decades have passed since Tozer first said it,

I'm afraid the jewel, in most places of our world, is still missing. And the tragedy is intensified by the fact that there aren't many even in ministry who seem to be looking for it. The jewel remains hidden.

That is nothing short of amazing. We are able to find the contents of an Egyptian tomb and identify the remains, as well as the possessions, of an ancient king, Tutankhamen. We are able to locate and photograph the *Titanic* that sank as far back as April 1912, though it rests two miles deep in the North Atlantic Ocean. We are even able to locate and bring to trial most, if not all, Nazi officers from Hitler's army. But we still can't seem to find the missing jewel of true worship. And good preaching—even doctrinal preaching—is no guarantee of worship. In fact, a strong pulpit often means weakness in worship. Peter Gillquist puts it this way:

> A common complaint I hear over and over again is, "I just don't get anything out of worship." Often that statement is accompanied by another: "Our pastor is the best Bible teacher I have ever heard. When the man opens the Scriptures, I really learn. But our church has no sense of worship." There almost appears to be a pattern: the churches that are strongest on the preaching of the Scriptures are often the weakest when it comes to worshiping and giving praise to the Lord. . . . People say they feel like bystanders.[1]

An equally convicting statement has been made by Robert Webber of Wheaton College:

> Worship is the weakest area of evangelical Christianity. We are strongest in the areas of evangelism, teaching, and fellowship. We are improving greatly in the area of servanthood (application of the gospel to social needs) and the ministry of healing (counseling and care for the emotional needs of people). But depth in the area of worship is badly lacking. We hardly know where to begin because we have lost nearly all contact with the past.[2]

Stop and think. Many of you travel much more than I do. You've been to other churches, as I have. You and I have been in formal churches, casual churches, Bible-teaching churches, evangelistic churches, beautiful churches, small, lovely, and even quaint churches. We have seen discipling churches, growing churches, dying churches, busy churches, renewal churches, denominational churches, independent churches; yes, even those that call themselves "New Testament churches." But chances are good we can count on both hands (with fingers left over) the churches we attended that were *worshiping* churches—places where we genuinely sensed the awesome presence of Almighty God.

I don't mean to sound spooky about this (it is a difficult concept to articulate). I am simply referring to a place where there was balance. A solid message from the Scriptures, and yet an accompanying blend of music and prayer and quietness that exalted the living God whom you came to worship. And along with all that, appropriate, distinct themes of thought conveyed through well-chosen words—freedom from clichés, without all the inane side comments and program hype that never fail to interrupt true worship. I am referring to places where we encountered the presence of the living God and found ourselves, as Wesley expressed it, "lost in wonder, love, and praise." Places where we truly could "worship the King all glorious above." Where we genuinely could "gratefully sing His power and His love." Where we could easily envision the Lord, high and lifted up as we sang, "Our Shield and Defender, the Ancient of Days, pavilioned in splendor and girded with praise."

When we find such places of worship, we have discovered a missing jewel.

Where are those rare gems?

Ten years after Tozer made that statement in Canada, I found myself in Fullerton, California, beginning a ministry at the First Evangelical Free Church. I am at a loss to describe all the things that drew me to this marvelous family, but looking back I realize that it was here I found the freedom, the openness, the spontaneity necessary to forge out a fresh theology of worship. I never announced such an agenda. I certainly had no book to turn to or some authority from whom I could receive counsel. I knew of no other church that was doing what I wanted to do. I didn't go out and find a few people to add to our staff who were "experts" in worship. Had I known of such, I probably would not have hired them, because "experts" were not what we needed.

At the risk of sounding terribly pious here, I wanted God alone to shape my theology of worship, as He had not done at any other place I had ever served. Somehow I knew music had to be woven into the scene—yet not to the exclusion of a consistently strong message from God's Book. Music and message had to blend if this jewel were going to be found in Fullerton. I wanted our church family to delight in the Lord Himself. Furthermore, I didn't want worship itself to become a god, an end in itself—an emotional shrine. I wanted God to be God. I wanted His Son to be preeminent in our assembly. And the only vehicle I knew to bring us to Him, at least in our large corporate gatherings, was worship.

Some pastors want programs. Some churches feature guest celebrities. Some ministers choose to highlight television, others add emphasis on service. I wanted our emphasis to be *worship*. I felt that alone would do more to motivate and deepen our commitment than any other single ingredient.

Some of the Fullerton flock have been with us all through those years. I remember when I introduced spontaneous a cappella singing. How different! Today such singing seems so important, so beautiful. But in those days, at least at the beginning of them, a few were afraid we were on our way to becoming a charismatic church. I still remember the letters and phone calls. Fear is such an enemy of worship! We are not a charismatic church, but I was convinced we could learn from our charismatic friends. Thankfully, the Fullerton folks trusted me. They were flexible enough to say, "Yes, let's do that." In fact, some even got so comfortable with those innovations that when we *didn't* try new things, they chided me (!), saying, "Where is that a cappella singing we've learned to love? Let's keep trying fresh things, Chuck." The family grew closer.

And along with that, we began to dovetail the Lord's table into a worship setting. And we gave music a far more significant role as we tied it together with the message from God's Book. How wrong to think of music as a "preliminary"! We began to weave singing into pastoral prayers, we developed a marvelous orchestra comprised of our own church family, and we began to bring the arts to the place where they belong, as an additional statement of worship. We even prayed through hymns and sang through our prayers. It became so enriching, so invigorating! The jewel began to sparkle as authentic worship replaced church meetings.

And all through the process of time, we were learning together. We made mistakes, and we shall in the future. But we were willing to flex. We were willing to shift and adapt and alter and change and give up and add to as we forged out fresh expressions of our praise. What were we doing? By means of fresh innovation and creative ideas, we were discovering the missing jewel! I never realized how much we were missing until we found it!

And now the one thing I fear, having come this far, is that somebody might plan to "package" it. You know, market the jewel. Once that starts, the spontaneity is lost and the Spirit is quenched. We haven't a corner on God's truth, nor a full understanding of what is involved in worship. All we know is this: We love our God. We want to express our praise and our adoration to Him freshly, fully, freely. We remain open to try new ideas, but our goal is always the same—to connect with the living Lord.

I have found that it is impossible to lead a group of people in something that is not a part of me personally. So I had to cultivate a *private* worship without talking about it, without spelling it out, without even confessing to the struggles of it. And I had to add to my discipline of prayer such things as meaningful times of singing, and to my walk with God quiet moments of silence. And even in the pressured times I had to work out a way for worship to fit. It was so delicate, even elusive.

Do you remember a line out of one of the songs in *The*

*Sound of Music*, sung by the Mother Superior? She did not know quite what to do with the young, creative, energetic Maria (played by Julie Andrews), so she asked, "How do you hold a moonbeam in your hand?" In many ways, the true, deep experience of worship is like trying to hold a moonbeam in your hand. There is no way you can define it or contain it—all you can do is let it shine. The same is true of worship.

I promised myself that if I ever wrote on doctrine, dealing with theology from a practical viewpoint, I would not conclude without addressing the importance of worship. And my suggestion to you regarding worship? Don't be afraid of it, don't ignore it. It's a moonbeam. Let it shine! Let it shine!

 *Extending Your Roots*

"A true, deep experience of worship is like trying to hold a moonbeam in your hand—all you can do is let it shine."

1.  Complete the acrostic using words that express your feelings about fellowshiping with God.

w
o
r
s
h
i
p

2.  Respond to these statements:
Worship is the missing jewel of the evangelical church.

True worship is an experience.

Every person worships something.

## Taproot

1. A beautiful scene of worship is painted for us in Isaiah 6. Let your imagination fill in between the lines. Why does worship focus on God?

2. What did God tell Isaiah to do?

3. Identify several hymns written from this Scripture passage. Read each hymn prayerfully.

4. What does God tell you to do?

# 21 The Missing Jewel Rediscovered

How am I to enter into the experience of worship . . . how am I to let it shine? I think I have found something of the answer, thanks to God's Book and God's family.

Tucked away in the hymnbook of our Bible, the Psalms, is a grand statement of invitation. I'd like us to think about that ancient hymn, Psalm 95, for just a few moments—to relive in our minds the truth that has been preserved for centuries.

If we struggle with the concept of worship as "too elusive," we must be equally concerned about making it too mechanical. I deliberately resist suggesting something like "Five Steps to Worship." Or, "Worship Made Easy—Here's How!" I have no plan to package it so that you are able to read this chapter, then pass along several "transferable concepts" of worship. But perhaps you will grasp what I'm driving at as you digest these thoughts. Like the Scottish people say, "Some things are better felt than telt."

I want you to "feel" what this is all about, according to Psalm 95. I want you to experience the emotions flowing from the psalmist's pen as you read this passage. By the way, if there are precision-minded engineers reading, please, please, don't take this psalm so literally. It's to be understood symbolically. And if you don't have the ability to do that, talk it over with your wife! I've met more wives who are poets than husbands. Let's see if this psalm will help us get a handle on the moonbeam called worship.

## Its Identity and Meaning

> O come, let us sing for joy to the Lord; Let us shout joyfully
> to the rock of our salvation. Let us come before His presence
> with thanksgiving; Let us shout joyfully to Him with psalms
> (vv. 1-2).

But why? Why should we come before our God with thanksgiving and joyful shouts? Why take the psalmist up on his
invitation? Because our God is great. He deserves our highest praise.

> For the Lord is a great God, and a great King above all
> gods, In whose hand are the depths of the earth; The peaks of
> the mountains are His also (vv. 3-4).

The psalmist interjects that illustration to show us the in-
finitude of our God. From the deepest place on earth, which
would be in the bottom of some sea, to the highest peak in
the Himalayan mountain range—earth's highest spot—
from depth to height, our God is greater. And Someone that
awesome, that great, is deserving of our silent praise as well
as our vocal praise and melodious praise and shouting
praise. Our God is great! He is above all other gods, He is
greater than the ear-splitting depths and the dizzy, tower-
ing heights.

> The sea is His, for it was He who made it; And His hands
> formed the dry land (v.5).

Have you been out at sea? I mean out in the midst of one of
earth's oceans? What awesome sights . . . how frightening
they can be!

I will never forget crossing the Pacific Ocean during my
days in the Marine Corps. Our troop ship seemed so enormous all the time it sat docked at San Diego. But once we got
out of the harbor and the farther out to sea we went, the
smaller we became. Until finally, at the heart of that vast
ocean, we felt like a flimsy matchstick. A storm struck,
which only added to my fears. When those swells reached
thirty to forty feet in height (the water was just as black as

the ace of spades), and the sky became filled with angry clouds, and the wind was howling, I gained a new respect for the sea. The bow of our ship drove into one swell after another as the ship sank and rose . . . sank and rose. A stinging blast of salty mist blew across the deck as cold ocean water swept over the decks. Talk about scared! My prayer life was enhanced on that ship.

It was there—in the midst of the raging Pacific Ocean—that I first found Psalm 139.

> If I take the wings of the dawn, If I dwell in the remotest part of the sea, Even there Thy hand will lead me, And Thy right hand will lay hold of me (vv. 9-10).

Why? Because the sea is His. He made it. Neither waves nor winds intimidate Him. There is no swell that causes our God to suck in His breath out of fear. There is no depth that causes Him to lift His eyebrows in amazement. He made it all! The vast sea is His. And the vast land masses were formed with His hands. How glorious He is in strength! How deserving of our respect! So we aren't surprised to read:

> Come, let us worship and bow down; Let us kneel before the Lord our Maker (Ps. 95:6).

The most basic meaning of worship is the thought of being on one's face. And to intensify such a position of abject submission, an ancient worshiper would kneel, place the palms of his hands on the ground, and remain in the prone position, with his face hidden before God. Try *that* sometime!

> For He is our God, And we are the people of His pasture, and the sheep of His hand (v. 7).

In worship we become preoccupied with the Lord. We don't watch something happen, we participate in it. It isn't like going to a ball game and seeing a few players knocking themselves out on a field. It's coming to a place in one's life, either alone, with a few, or with many, where one "connects" with the living God. It is almost as though you could reach out and touch Him.

The best definition I've come up with, and perhaps the

one with the fewest words, is this: *Worship is a human response to a divine revelation.* God has said something, and I respond to it. God is doing things, and I respond to them. On occasion, the appropriate response may be absolute silence as we meditate on our God. On other occasions the best response may be in the loudest possible voice of praise. It may be as you drink in the majestic strains of a pipe organ.

Just yesterday, sitting in the worship center of our church and listening to the moving strains of a hymn being played on our pipe organ, I "connected." You will understand better if I mention the lyrics:

> Like a river glorious Is God's perfect peace,
> Over all victorious In its bright increase;
> Perfect, yet it floweth Fuller every day,
> Perfect, yet it groweth Deeper all the way.
>
> Stayed upon Jehovah, Hearts are fully blest;
> Finding, as He promised, Perfect peace and rest.[1]

I felt it. The message passed through my mind. At that moment I was lost in the wonder and praise of my God. I could envision a river, with its mysterious currents, moving and deep. I could sense the peace, I could feel the rest and relief from all anxiety.

An amazing thing about worship is that you don't care what anybody else thinks. You couldn't care less what someone else thinks about you as your heart is lifted up in profound awe. Seems like everything else is blocked out as you are being "touched" by God. Yes, touched—not literally, but symbolically, figuratively. How important is touch!

Several months ago I heard about a man who sat in coffee shops all over the world and watched people. He was conducting an experiment on touch. He counted the times people touched each other during an hour's span. He kept a record of his observations, and his observations were revealing. In Puerto Rico there were one hundred and eighty touches an hour in the coffee shop. In France it was reduced to one hundred and ten an hour. When he came to America, it dropped amazingly to only *two times an hour*. In England, not even once! When I heard that, I thought to myself, *He should have gone to Italy, ohhh!* I often say to people, "Italians don't simply hug and kiss you, they *frisk* you." I mean, they are all over you. I love it! Those Italian meals—aren't they the greatest experiences in the world? Food is flying, words are flying, arms are flying. There is laughter, openness, such fun! A real Italian meal is sort of a survival of the fittest. They're touching like crazy. I don't believe I've ever been around a true Italian who didn't touch.

I wonder how many Italian Christians really worship? You see, it isn't simply touching one another, though there's nothing wrong with that. It is being open and willing. One of the greatest hindrances to worship is resistance to *anyone* touching me. Some Christians don't want anyone to touch them, to probe their personal affairs. That is often blocked off. But you see, in worship, there is no place that is free from His touch. Resistance pushes Him away. And so worship is a response—an active, open, unguarded response to God, whereby we declare His worth in an intimate manner, leaving Him room to touch us, to flood us with His peaceful presence.

## Its Significance and Purpose

Let's leave Psalm 95 and give some thought to several reasons worship is so significant. What happens when that "connection" occurs? Whether it's in a gathering of thousands, or when I'm alone in a closet of prayer with Him, or perhaps with a few, what happens?

*1. Worship magnifies my God.* All else is eclipsed in His presence.

*2. Worship enlarges my horizons.* I begin to see beyond the self-imposed fences.

*3. Worship eclipses my fears.* I soon forget those things that gnaw at me when I worship.

*4. Worship changes my perspective.* It is nothing short of remarkable. An attitude on Friday is so different from on a

Monday, because sandwiched between a Friday and a Monday is a worship service in which my whole perspective changes.

I was leaving a worship service late one evening several Sundays ago. I had parked my pickup alongside the curb. One of my friends spotted it as he was leaving the meeting and tucked a brief note under the windshield wiper. At first my stomach turned when I saw something under my windshield wiper. But when I realized it was a note, I stopped right then and read it. It spoke of a change of perspective that had occurred in his life. It wasn't something I had done or said. I can change no one's perspective. It wasn't the mortar, or the brick, or the carpet, or the pulpit, or the sound system. It was the living God who had invaded that man's life and touched him deeply in his churning place and calmed his spirit. And he didn't know anything better to do than to thank one of the people who had been present at the same experience of worship. I understood. He was refreshed, which brings me to the fifth reason worship is so significant.

*5. Worship refreshes my spirit.* How can we possibly describe this?

*6. Worship enhances my work.* When I put worship to work in my life, when I see worship as a response to God woven through the fabric of my day, it's amazing how my attitude toward tasks changes. Life takes on a melodious dimension that sets our hearts to singing.

At this point I have to say more about music. I must address it. Few things bring out the beauty of worship like music. God gave us song! His longest book in Scripture is the ancient psalter—the hymns of the Hebrews. Then why are we so resistant to giving it a prominent place, especially music centering its message on the Word of God? As I stated earlier, music is not simply a "preliminary." Music is not tacked on. Nor is it a "filler." It's not something we do while getting ready for the important part. By the way, I cannot say enough about the importance of having just the right person giving leadership to the church in the realm of music. I have one of the very best in Howie Stevenson, but there are other great ones available. And I suggest that we not view these gifted people simply as "song leaders," but as *worship* leaders. A worshiping church is a singing church, since music is vital to worship. In fact, Psalm 92 begins:

> It is good to give thanks to the Lord, And to sing praises to Thy name, O Most High; To declare Thy lovingkindness in the morning, And Thy faithfulness by night, With the ten-stringed lute, and with the harp; With resounding music upon the lyre. For Thou, O Lord, hast made me glad by what Thou hast done, I will sing for joy at the works of Thy hands (vv. 1-4).

I wonder why it is that the song has dried up in our voices? Why are there so few who sing, including the pastors . . . I mean really sing heartily to the Lord with full voice. Stop and consider. I wouldn't doubt if fewer people than ever sing in the shower any more. How many of you in a business or profession hear your partner humming a song? How many do you see singing out joyfully on a freeway? (Now that's a new one.) No wonder our singing is limited to Sunday! I have asked myself—why?

I've come up with a couple of answers.

*The pressures of life squeeze out our song.* Song requires a free spirit within—creativity, relaxation, freedom from tension. But so many live their lives in submission to that pressure, the song is squeezed out of them. What a loss!

*Someone else sings for us.* You get in the car, on goes the radio with its blaring music. There is background music in our offices, in our homes, even on airplanes, in grocery stores and department stores; they all have "mood" songs. There's piped music in restaurants. And would you believe in elevators? You can't even be alone to hum a little tune to yourself in an elevator without this dumb elevator music coming through. Why? I had a flight attendant tell me it was to deaden people's fears. I don't know about that . . . some of that music is pretty scary by itself.

Let me encourage you to start singing again. Yes, even when you're alone. Add it to your time with God. Get up with a song, not someone else's song. Before anything in the day has a chance to squeeze it out of you, express your praise in a song. If you can't create one, find a hymnbook. Buy one for your own use. Use it. Right along with your time in God's Book, sing the songs back to Him.

 *Extending Your Roots*

The moonbeam called worship has shone on many places where individuals or groups connected with God. Read each reference and notice how worship was involved or could have applied.

*1. Altars*

Genesis 4:3-4; 8:20-22; 12:7-10; 26:23-25; 28:11-22
Exodus 17:14-16; Joshua 22:26-27.

*2. The Tabernacle*

Exodus 25—31. Read God's instructions for building the tabernacle. Read the verses and list instructions applying to worship. Locate a picture of the tabernacle. Read Leviticus 21:4-6 and notice some of God's requirements for worship leaders.

### 3. The Temple

1 Chronicles 22. Trace references to the temple through the Old and New Testament.

### 4. Synagogue

Matthew 6:5; 12:9-13; Luke 4:15-23; Acts 6:7,9; 14:1.

### 5. The Early Church

Acts 2:41-47; Romans 16:5; 1 Corinthians 16:19; Colossians 4:15; Philemon 2.

 *Taproot*

1. Peter, James, and John accepted an important invitation from Jesus. Read Mark 9:2-13. As a result of this worship experience, the apostles learned or rediscovered some things.

(1) They began to understand what Jesus had been teaching.

*Growing Deep in the Christian Life: The Family of God*

(2) They learned who Jesus really was.

(3) They rediscovered what God was like.

Think about a special time when you really worshiped Jesus. Or a time when you rediscovered some truths about God. How did that worship experience strengthen your faith?

2. Listed below is a traditional order of worship for churches. Read the outline and plan a worship service to meet your worship needs.

*Prelude*
*Call to worship*
*Hymn*
*Prayer*
*Responsive reading*
*Special music*
*Hymn*
*Offering*
*Choir special*
*Scripture reading*
*Sermon*
*Invitation*
*Benediction*
*Postlude*

3. Share your idea with a person responsible for planning the worship service in your church.

# 22 Some Often-Overlooked Facets of the Jewel

There are at least three facets of the missing jewel of worship that are easily overlooked. By my mentioning them, perhaps you may find fresh motivation to cultivate a greater love for worship.

*1. Worship is sought by God.* John 4 tells the story of Jesus speaking to the woman at the well:

> You worship that which you do not know, we worship that which we know, for salvation is from the Jews. But an hour is coming, and now is, when the true worshipers shall worship the Father in spirit and truth; for such people the Father seeks to be His worshipers (vv. 22-23).

I appreciate Professor Zane Hodges' comment: "This utterance on worship is timeless and absolutely definitive. The time has come!" For what? For true worshipers to worship God! But have you ever noticed the two essential ingredients?

> God is spirit; and those who worship Him must worship in spirit and truth (v. 24).

Our worship *must* be in keeping with the revealed Word of God. That's truth, the Bible. And our worship *must* be in spirit.

Now this is where things tend to get a little sticky and hard to describe. Spirit is in the unseen realm. It probably would include the realm of imagination—mental pictures in our inner connection between His Spirit and our spirit.

To appreciate a great piece of music by Beethoven or Bach, I am not required to read the score. But I do have to enter into the feeling of that music. I have to let it capture me. I have to be open to that. In order for me to enter into the spirit of a song done by the church choir, or by some fine soloist, or through a statement of praise given in testimony, I have to enter unguarded into the *spirit* of that moment—without resistance. I say again, as long as I am resistant to such a thing, I will not enter into the depth of worship. I *must* worship in spirit!

Frequently, I find that I am in the midst of people who are afraid of feelings. Most often I find this among Bible-believing evangelicals, the more rigid brand. The same ones who are in love with the truth are often afraid of the spirit, so fearful of being carried to an extreme, they won't even let a little crack appear in the door of their emotions. The consequence is nothing short of tragic: sterile, cold truth without the warmth of feelings. And worship takes a backseat. I find few settings more uncomfortable.

May I give a word of encouragement to seminaries today? Most of the men and women who study in theological graduate schools don't arrive at those institutions with an understanding of worship. I encourage you who serve in such places to help your students leave differently. I suggest you commit yourself to introduce to each seminarian a primary understanding of the basics of what worship is about. His or her theological training is incomplete without such a grasp. How? Start at the most obvious place—the chapel. Cultivate a chapel service marked by quality—fine music, good speakers (even if it means having fewer chapels), with a constant emphasis on quality worship. You might invite worship leaders to visit your campus a time or two each year. Include the ministers of music as well. Expose your ministers-in-the-making to those outstanding models. What a contribution to make on young lives! Especially since worship is sought by God.

2. *Worship has been practiced in the past.* If I had the time to trace where worship appears in history, according to Scripture, I could literally take you from Genesis to Revelation. Do you know the first appearance of worship in the

Bible? It will surprise you. The first time worship is mentioned is in Genesis 22 when Abraham is about to sacrifice his son Isaac on the altar. The old patriarch says to his friends down at the base of the mountain:

> Stay here with the donkey, and I and the lad will go yonder; and we will *worship* and return to you (v. 5, emphasis mine).

If we consider Job in the same context of the patriarchs, the suffering saint mentioned worship after he lost everything. Sitting in sackcloth and ashes he said:

> Naked I came from my mother's womb, And naked I shall return there. The Lord gave and the Lord has taken away. Blessed be the name of the Lord (Job 1:21).

Prior to that confession the text says, "Then Job arose and tore his robe and shaved his head, and he fell to the ground and worshiped (v. 20).

Yes, it's possible to worship on a hospital bed. It is possible to worship though bankrupt, bruised, and beaten. Worship doesn't require comfortable surroundings, organ music, and the soft seats of a church pew. You don't have to have an orchestra. Those things may help enhance it, but worship is just as appropriate when we are all alone with our thoughts, as Abraham and Job were.

You may think I'm weird, but when I look at the fluid lines on a Michelangelo piece of sculpture, and I take the time to study that eight-foot masterpiece of white marble depicting David, I worship my God. He gave the genius that gift. He, through the hands of that gifted artist, sculpted that statue for us to appreciate. When I hear the loving strains of a hymn, I worship. I'm not worshiping the hymn, or the player, or the singer. I am worshiping God, the Giver. There are dozens of such experiences awaiting our worship.

*3. Worship is needed in the present.* Turn to Romans 12. Worship is not only something to be enjoyed as a recipient, it is something to *do* as a participant. That is my whole chapter in one statement. Worship is not dreamy and passive. It is a verb. Action is in the term.

> I urge you therefore, brethren, by the mercies of God, to present your bodies a living and holy sacrifice, acceptable to God, which is your spiritual service of worship (v. 1).

Do you serve on a board or a committee in your church? Believe it or not, that's to be an experience of worship. Do you teach a class of children or teenagers or adults? That is your worship . . . your "spiritual service of worship." Do you sing in a choir? Do you play an instrument in the church orchestra? Do you sing as a soloist or as a part of an ensemble? That is a statement of worship as you minister the gospel to others. Do you work behind the scenes, not seen by the public, as you give time to youth or to adults or to children? That is your worship. Do you give regularly to the work of God? Is your giving marked by sacrifice and consistency? Do you realize God calls that your "spiritual service of worship"?

It will revolutionize your whole concept of Christian service if you begin to think of your involvement as an act of worship.

## *Extending Your Roots*

### W _ R _ H _ P

1. Is something missing from your personal or corporate worship? Perhaps you need to take a closer look at some of the major doctrines presented in this study series. Because worship is needed in the present, let's take another look at some opportunities for worship. Think of several ways you or your church could worship using the suggested doctrines. Write down your ideas.

*The Holy Scripture*
- singing the Word

*God*
- praising Him

*Man*
- reading about creation

*The Church*
- singing hymns

*Baptism and the Lord's Supper*
- planning creative ways to participate

*Jesus*
- obeying His commands

*Holy Spirit*
- allowing Him to empower the worship service

*Salvation*
- reading psalms

*Family of God*
- strengthening fellowship

2. I will practice some of these worship ideas in my life beginning:

*Growing Deep in the Christian Life: The Family of God*

## Taproot

1. The apostle John witnessed the events reported in Revelation. Read Revelation 22:8-9. Who is to be worshiped?

2. Read the following psalms and list ways you can worship God in the present.
Psalm 8; 19; 27; 29; 150.

3. Just for fun, play a Christian tape of instrumental music and read aloud these "songs" from the Psalms. You will worship!

# 23 | Sparkling Beauty of the Rediscovered Jewel

A. W. Tozer was right. Worship has been the missing jewel of the evangelical church. But I would like to add: It need not *remain* missing. Let's make a difference! Let's risk innovating—let's cultivate a renewed appreciation for and participation in active, fulfilling worship. I love the way my friend, Dr. Ron Allen, refers to worship as our celebration of God. Read his words thoughtfully.

What, then, is the essence of worship? It is the celebration of God! When we worship God, *we celebrate Him:* We extol Him, we sound His praises, we boast in Him.

Worship is not the casual chatter that occasionally drowns out the organ prelude; we celebrate God when we allow the prelude to attune our hearts to the glory of God by the means of the music.

Worship is not the mumbling of prayers or the mouthing of hymns with little thought and less heart; we celebrate God when we join together earnestly in prayer and intensely in song.

Worship is not self-aggrandizing words or boring clichés when one is asked to give a testimony; we celebrate God when all of the parts of the service fit together and work to a common end.

Worship is not grudging gifts or compulsory service; we celebrate God when we give to Him hilariously and serve Him with integrity.

Worship is not haphazard music done poorly, not even great music done merely as a performance; we celebrate God when we enjoy and participate in music to His glory.

Worship is not a distracted endurance of the sermon; we

147

celebrate God as we hear His Word gladly and seek to be conformed by it more and more to the image of our Savior.

Worship is not a sermon that is poorly prepared and carelessly delivered; we celebrate God when we honor His Word with our words, by His Spirit.

Worship is not the hurried motions of a "tacked-on" Lord's Table; we celebrate God pre-eminently when we fellowship gratefully at the ceremonial meal that speaks so centrally of our faith in the Christ Who dies for us, Who rose again on our behalf, and Who is to return for our good.

As a thoughtful gift is a celebration of a birthday, as a special evening out is a celebration of an anniversary, as a warm eulogy is a celebration of a life, as a sexual embrace is a celebration of a marriage—*so a worship service is a celebration of God.*[1]

Finally, let me ask you three probing questions that examine the jewel in your personal life.

*1. Does your public worship sparkle with creativity and variety?* If you want that to happen, start letting the hymn speak to you. Allow your mind to meditate on the piece that's being played, even the prelude, the offertory, the postlude. Allow yourself to enter into the music, considering the words if you know them, praying your own words if you don't. Let the sparkle return. Let is shine!

*2. Does your private worship sparkle with quality and consistency?* Years ago, I was working closely with a man who was trying to help me understand private worship. He went through a very, very low time in his life. I went by his home one afternoon to find him, and he wasn't there. His wife said, "I think he's down at the office." It had begun to rain. By the time I got to his office down in the center of town, it was pouring—rain was really splashing down.

I made my way around the corner to this little, inauspicious office where he met with God. Before I saw him, I could hear him. I could hear him singing. He was singing the lines from that great hymn, "Come Thou Fount of Every Blessing."

I stood alone in the darkness and the rain, listening . . . pondering the truth I heard.

> Prone to wander, Lord, I feel it,
> Prone to leave the God I love;
> Here's my heart, Lord , take and seal it,
> Seal it for Thy courts above.[2]

As I stood outside that little bamboo shack, seeing the flicker of the candle in his room, I felt I was standing on sacred soil. His private worship was obvious to me. And I walked away having learned more in that brief moment than I could have learned in a year of instruction. I shall never forget his model. He worshiped publicly because he worshiped privately.

3. *Has something taken the sparkle out of your worship?* If so, it's time to do some soul searching. Probe deeply. Whatever it is that is stealing your joy and sucking the life out of your worship must be removed. Until that happens, I must warn you, you will continue to do little more than play church on Sundays. Anne Ortlund admits:

> When I was little we used to play church. We'd get the chairs into rows, fight over who'd be preacher, vigorously lead the hymn singing, and generally have a great carnal time.
>
> The aggressive kids naturally wanted to be up front, directing or preaching. The quieter ones were content to sit and be entertained by the up-fronters.
>
> Occasionally we'd get mesmerized by a true sensationalistic crowd-swayer—like the girl who said, "Boo! I'm the Holy Ghost!" But in general, if the up-fronters were pretty good they could hold their audience quite a while. If they weren't so good, eventually the kids would drift off to play something else—like jump rope or jacks.
>
> Now that generation has grown up, but most of them haven't changed too much. Every Sunday they still play church. They line up in rows for the entertainment. If it's pretty good, their church may grow. If it's not too hot, eventually they'll drift off to play something else—like yachting or wife swapping.[3]

Yes, Anne is right. All the stuff we do in place of true worship is a cheap substitute. It doesn't satisfy. It certainly doesn't sparkle.

If you love God, if you love His Word, if you love the doctrines revealed in His Word, then I encourage you to become an active participant in worship. Find the jewel and let it shine! Let it shine!

## Extending Your Roots

1. Have you ever thought about what happens to you when you rediscover true worship? Consider these:

- You enjoy God more.
- You see the real you.
- You learn to pray.
- You become what God created you to be.
- The Holy Spirit becomes your helper.
- You learn to trust Jesus more.

2. Can you locate in Scripture a promise to support each of these evidences of true worship?

## Taproot

1. Public worship is our celebration of God. Complete the following evaluation of your church worship service. Rate yourself with a:

yes plus (the best)
yes minus (not bad)
no plus (acceptable)
no minus (Help!)

_____ Our worship services are friendly and make visitors feel welcome.

_____ Our congregational singing includes a good balance of music for youth, baby boomers, median adults, and senior adults.

_____ Our members feel refreshed and renewed in the Lord as they leave.

_____ The Holy Spirit *can* change the order of service.

_____ The Lord's Supper is specifically planned for worship.

_____ Special emphases on worship are planned in advance.

_____ Our church offers a time of meditation for members to prepare for worship.

_____ Testimonies during the worship are given careful consideration.

What grade do you give your church worship?

2. How can you help your church rediscover the celebration of God?

# Conclusion

I have two reactions, now that we have come to the end. *Whew!* and *Why?*

The first is an expression of exhaustion. What began as a rather simple and easy approach to the doctrines that lie at the roots of our faith evolved into a project that has required an enormous amount of discipline and determination. The tough part was maintaining relevance and practicality with each subject. Now I understand why most books on doctrine focus on theory, include long lists of Bible verses, employ a lot of scholarly jargon, and give little attention to the *application* of theological issues. It's easier that way!

I was tempted to opt for the theoretical approach at times, but I'm glad I didn't yield. The hard work, I think, paid off. I'm tired tonight, but my joy comes in imagining how the Lord is going to use these pages in the lives of some who would normally be disinterested and turned off by the oversized, stuffy-looking volumes on doctrine.

As I said at the beginning, my wish has not been to impress those who are already sharp, well-informed students of systematic theology. Nor has it been to exhaust every issue on the doctrinal spectrum. My deep desire has been to address some of the major points of interest in a way that would be interesting, understandable, and true to Scripture, especially for the uninitiated. I hope I have succeeded. If so, the *Whew!* on my lips will become a *Wow!* on someone else's. Nothing would please me more.

Of greater importance is the second reaction: *Why?* This is a question of purpose. Why have I taken your time and invested my energy doing spade work around these old roots

beneath this giant tree? In a society that is so forward looking and technologically advanced, why is it important to return to our roots? I have been asking myself this "Why"
question all the way through this study series. It has been
the answer that has kept me at the task.

Why? Because we are fast becoming a rootless generation
that is giving less respect to those people who shaped our
faith and less regard to those truths that solidify it. Riding
on the highs and lows of emotional waves, many (most?) are
awash in an uncertain sea that lacks biblical guidelines,
moral absolutes, historical breadth, and doctrinal depth.
We have become dogmatic about the value of wings and
dreams, but embarrassingly soft on roots and truth.

Substance—time-honored biblical content—is increasingly conspicuous by its absence. Far too many in God's family
have minds like beds which need to be made and remade
rather regularly.

We need to be absolutely sure of certain things.

I'm not suggesting that we become closed-minded and
stubborn, but at the same time we dare not live like little
children "tossed here and there by waves, and carried about
by every wind of doctrine" (Eph. 4:14). We must cultivate
more than just the ability to get along well with one another. Relationships, as significant as they are, have come dan-
gerously close to replacing a knowledge of the holy.

How we feel and what we think are now considered more
important than what God wants and what His Word says.
At the nucleus of today's philosophy of life is a me-ism none
can deny. The "I" has taken the place of "Thou." Because
we adults have sown the wind, our young are sure to reap
the whirlwind.

This was brought home rather forcefully in a one-page article entitled "The Modern Mount Rushmore." The author,
Ralph Schoenstein, humorously yet pointedly presents
proof of this from a classroom he visited:

My daughter Lori, who is eight, told me last night that she
wants to grow up to sing like either Judy Garland or Michael

Jackson. "Try for Judy Garland," I said. "A girl needs a great soprano to be Michael Jackson."

These two singers have become Lori's first hero and heroine. They are hardly figures for commemorative stamps, but many children have no heroes or heroines anymore, no noble achievers they yearn to emulate. . . . One day last spring I stood before 20 children of eight and nine in Lori's third-grade class to see if any heroes or heroines were inspiring them. I asked each child to give me the names of the three greatest people he had ever heard about.

"Michael Jackson, Brooke Shields and Boy George," said a small blond girl, giving me one from all three sexes.

"Michael Jackson, Spider-Man and God," a boy then said, naming a new holy trinity.

. . . When the other children recited, Michael Jackson's name was spoken again and again, but Andrew Jackson never, nor Washington, Lincoln or any other presidential immortal. Just Ronald Reagan, who made it twice, once behind Batman and once behind Mr. T., a hero who likes to move people by saying, "Sucker, I'll break your face." . . . And I heard no modern equivalent of Charles A. Lindbergh, America's beloved "Lone Eagle." . . .

In answer to my request for heroes, I had expected to hear such names as Michael Jackson, Mr. T., Brooke Shields and Spider-Man from the kids, but I had not expected the replies of the eight who answered "Me." Their heroes were themselves.

It is sad enough to see the faces on Mount Rushmore replaced by rock stars, brawlers and cartoons, but it is sadder still to see Mount Rushmore replaced by a mirror.[1]

When I first read those words, I thought of the analogy in Scripture that refers to our looking in a mirror. What is interesting is that the biblical writer pleads for a replacement of the mirror with the truth of God, which he calls "the word implanted."

Therefore putting aside all filthiness and all that remains of wickedness, in humility receive the word implanted, which is able to save your souls. But prove yourselves doers of the word, and not merely hearers who delude themselves. For if any one is a hearer of the word and not a doer, he is

*Conclustion*

like a man who looks at his natural face in a mirror; for once he has looked at himself and gone away, he has immediately forgotten what kind of person he was. But one who looks intently at the perfect law, the law of liberty, and abides by it, not having become a forgetful hearer but an effectual doer, this man shall be blessed in what he does (Jas. 1:21-25).

My immediate hope is that you have found enough solid substance in these chapters to whet your appetite for further digging around these roots. My ultimate hope is that you would not only look intently but that you would *abide* by these things. My fear is that you might become more fascinated with individual roots than the whole tree, and more intrigued by the hearing of the Word than involved in the doing of it.

That is why I have suggested ways to keep the doctrines out of the realm of sterile theory and in touch with the real world. Let us *never* forget that our Lord's goal for us is that we become people who obey, not merely study—Christians who yield our wills in greater obedience, not merely expand our minds for greater intelligence.

I don't make many absolute promises, but there is one I can make without hesitation. If you will devote yourself to a consistent study of the Scriptures, balancing doctrinal intake with practical applications of the truth, your life will take on new meaning. Furthermore, I can promise you that knowledge will replace ignorance and superstition. The mirror of me-ism will be broken by an unselfish spirit. Stability will return, displacing uncertainty and fear. And a depth you have never had before will mark your life, instead of superficiality and shallowness.

As important as wings and dreams may be, what we really need is a solid network of roots. Hopefully, this volume has convinced you that growing deep in the Christian life is not optional, it's essential.

By returning to our roots, we can become like that tree the psalmist mentions. It is a strong, stable tree, firmly planted by streams of water . . . one that yields seasonal fruit and has no withering leaves—one that stand the test of time, reaching full and enviable maturity.

# Notes

## Part I

### Chapter 3

1. Gloria Gaither, "The Family of God," © 1970. Used by permission.

### Chapter 7

1. Dr. Paul Brand and Philip Yancey, *Fearfully and Wonderfully Made* (Grand Rapids, Mich.: Zondervan, 1980), 59-60.

### Chapter 8

1. Judith Viorst, *If I Were in Charge of the World and Other Worries* (New York: Atheneum, 1981), 2-3.

### Chapter 9

1. William Pitts, "The Little Brown Church," *The American Song Book* (New York: Robbins Music Corporation, 1942), 91.

### Chapter 13

1. Bill and Gloria Gaither and Don Marsh, "God Has Always Had a People," *The Church Triumphant* (Alexandria, Ind.: Paragon/Gaither). Used by permission.

## Part II

### Chapter 15

1. Armen Keteyian, "Nobody Wanted to Believe What Happened," *Sports Illustrated*, 9 September 1985, 10.

### Chapter 16

1. William Barclay, *More New Testament Words* (New York: Harper & Brother, 1958), 134-35.
2. Ken Medema, "If This Is Not a Place," © 1977. Used by permission.

### Chapter 17

1. Gordon MacDonald, *The Effective Father* (Wheaton Ill.: Tyndale House, 1977), 68-69.

### Chapter 18

1. Lawrence Crabb and Dan Allender, *Encouragement: The Key to Caring* (Grand Rapids, Mich.: Zondervan, 1984), 121-23.
2. Billy Graham, *How to Be Born Again* (Waco, Tex.: Word Books, 1977), 11, 119, 120-21.

### Chapter 20

1. Peter E. Gillquist, *The Physical Side of Being Spiritual* (Grand Rapids, Mich.: Zondervan, 1979), 115.
2. Robert E. Webber, Foreword to *Praise! A Matter of Life and Breath*, Ronald Barclay Allen (Nashville: Thomas Nelson, 1980), 9.

### Chapter 21

1. Frances R. Havergal, "Like a River Glorious."

### Chapter 23

1. Ronald Allen, *Worship: Rediscovering the Missing Jewel* (Portland, Ore.: Multnomah Press, 1982), 18-19.
2. Robert Robinson, "Come, Thou Fount," © 1966 Singspiration. Used by permission.
3. Anne Ortlund, *Up with Worship* (Glendale, Calif.: Regal Books Division G/L Publications, 1975), 2-3.

### Conclusion

1. Ralph Schoenstein, "The Modern Mount Rushmore," *Newsweek*, 6 August, 1984.